"For Dr. Fletcher, the motto of a 24/7 Christian should be 'the undivided life is worth living!' In order to live such a life—and to bridge the gap between Baptism's universal call to holiness and the frenetic pace of everyday life—lay men and women must begin to see the Gospel story as *their* story. A prayer life rooted in the Scriptures will empower the Catholic lay faithful to answer the call of missionary discipleship in their secular vocations. *24/7 Christian* offers tools for discerning one's personal calling, as well as inspiration for responding with humility and joy."

—David D. Spesia
The Diocese of Joliet's Secretary for Evangelization and Catechesis

24/7 Christian

The Secular Vocation of the Laity

Christine M. Fletcher

LITURGICAL PRESS
Collegeville, Minnesota

www.litpress.org

1   2   3   4   5   6   7   8   9

Library of Congress Cataloging-in-Publication Data

Fletcher, Christine M.
    24/7 Christian : the secular vocation of the laity / Christine M. Fletcher.
       pages   cm
    Includes bibliographical references.
    ISBN 978-0-8146-4968-8 — ISBN 978-0-8146-4993-0 (ebook)
    1. Christian life—Catholic authors.   I. Title.

BX2350.3.F55   2015
248.4'82—dc23   2014033118

Contents

Preface

Roger was a physician who was the head of his practice group. He was working between 60 and 90 hours a week. He constantly felt stressed: his job meant that he had little time for anything other than work; his family was coming a distant second. He made it to Mass most weekends but felt that he could no longer be involved in the parish or in his community.

Tom was a CEO who had turned around a mid-sized company that had been engaged in unethical practices. He got rid of the malefactors, created a new healthy, ethical, culture, and developed new product lines that benefited the economy, reducing energy costs for consumers and running expenses for colleges and universities. He wanted to work in a soup kitchen to "really live my faith."

Marsha was a stay-at-home wife and mother who was one of the mainstays of the parish. She taught in the religious education program, helped with the music ministry, was active in the Mothers' Circle and Women's Club. She was so involved with the parish that she had little time for anything except the parish and her family. She was concerned that she wasn't involved in the neighborhood or her children's schools. Her children had friends from many other faiths, and Marsha didn't know how to connect with them or their parents.

Sandra was a state representative and on the fast track in her state's politics. She found herself in disagreement with some Catholics on some social issues, such as welfare, and with other politicians on other life issues. The strain of balancing her work, her family, and her faith was getting harder and harder. She wasn't sure if she should continue, or just get out of politics.

Roger, Tom, Marsha, and Sandra all suffered from a divided life. Faith and life seemed to be in separate compartments. All of them needed to see their whole life as their Christian life and witness; they needed wholeness and holiness. Their offering to God consisted of their many obligations, all done for the love of Christ. Tom's idea of working in a soup kitchen was right and laudable; but he also needed to understand how his secular work was part of his Christian vocation. Mary's work in the parish was a great service, but she was not bringing the Good News to her neighbors who weren't Catholic. Sandra's life in politics seemed far from her faith, but she was serving an important role for the common good. Roger's life was out of balance; he knew his work was part of his vocation, but he could see that other areas of his life were suffering from lack of time and attention.

This book is for people like them who want to live their faith 24/7—at home, at work, in the community, and in the parish. Living our faith is both our vocation and our mission. *Vocation* comes from the Latin work for "call"; God calls us to love and serve him. We serve him by telling others about God's love. This is our *mission*, which comes from the Latin word for "being sent." When we talk about the two parts together—God's call and our response—we are talking about being disciples or followers of Christ. We may have been raised to think that vocation meant the special call to becoming a priest or a religious. It is true that each of us needs to choose a state in life, whether that be priesthood, religious life, marriage or single life. However, this choice is only one part of our vocation. Through baptism every Christian has the vocation to become a saint.

If we have chosen the lay state in life, we live out the call to holiness in the secular world. The Second Vatican Council states that "the laity, by their very vocation, seek the kingdom of God by engaging in temporal affairs and by ordering them to the plan of God. They live in the world, that is, in each and in all of the secular professions and occupations. They live in the ordinary circumstances of family and social life. . . . They are called there by God" (*Lumen Gentium* 31). Fifty years after the council, it is an appropriate time to reflect on the teachings that council gave us, especially those about the lay vocation. Lay life in the world has been one of the less studied parts of the council. Yet that teaching is a beacon of hope for anyone seeking a unified, whole life in which every aspect of life serves God.

This book will explore Scripture and the teaching of the council about the laity in the world in order to learn how to live this vocation today. Since each of us is a unique creation, this book will then look at discerning our particular gifts and talents. Finally, this book will look at practices from the Rule of St. Benedict that help us live out our vocation and our prayer, the foundation of our Christian life.

Chapter 1, "Faith and Life," looks at the church/world split and how it developed. Most Catholics now do not remember living in the Catholic ghetto, but the legacy of that time is still with us. We will see how the "world" means God's good creation, but it also means a creation marked by sin that presents us with difficult decisions in which good Catholics may disagree. We will also look at the particular challenges we face when we try to live our faith in our globalized consumer culture.

Chapter 2, "God Calls Us in Scripture," looks at Scripture, the primary source of our faith where we meet Jesus. Reading, studying, and meditating on Scripture is an essential step in discerning our particular call throughout our lives. The Gospel of Mark is especially important here because it is a gospel of discipleship, written for believers suffering persecution. The gospel shows how difficult the path of discipleship is, even for those who were Christ's closest companions. It is helpful to remember how often Peter and the apostles failed, yet Peter is our model because he didn't give up; when he was wrong, he admitted it and repented. Imitating Peter is the path to life, but it requires us to be humble and know ourselves as sinners.

The gospels also give us insight into how Jesus called ordinary people to be his followers and how he dealt with the outsiders of his day. Jesus lived in a multicultural, multifaith environment, more similar to our own than to the Catholic ghetto of years past. His encounters with the pagans and other outsiders show us a way to act in our own multifaith world. Finally, the gospels teach us how wealth is a temptation and show us God's values.

Chapter 3, "Vatican II: The Council and the Laity," will look at the new understanding of the lay vocation from the Second Vatican Council. The council highlighted the call of all Christians to holiness in their baptism, providing a new way of understanding our role in a changed world. This chapter recounts the changed understanding of the laity that emerged from the council as the fathers brought the riches of our tradition into dialogue with the new things of our culture. The documents of the council empower us as laity within the church by recognizing our freedom of conscience and of autonomous action in the world. This freedom carries a responsibility to see things with the eyes of Christ and to love God and our neighbor here and now.

Chapter 4, "Discovering My Call," looks at how we find our particular, individual call. We look at our personality, talents, values, goals, and stage of life. We stop to listen to what others have to tell us about ourselves, our gifts, and our needs. Joy should be the distinguishing mark of the Christian, and our work should be a place where, most of the time, we find fulfillment and satisfaction. Of course we also need to discern those times when we are asked to take up our cross and maybe do work that is dull, repetitive, and difficult, or suffer illness, weakness, and need. This process of discernment is lifelong, as we move through various stages and commitments. We want to bring our entire life—family, work, politics, church, civil society—into a unity of love and service to the Lord.

Chapter 5, "Living a 24/7 Christian Life," puts our vocation into the context of the Rule of St. Benedict. For 1500 years Benedict's wisdom has helped people end the divisions in their lives by bringing their souls and outward lives into alignment—and it remains a relevant guide even today. Benedict has perennial wisdom to teach us to move out of our selfishness and isolation and into community, especially through the practices of humility, stewardship, and a life lived in balance. Here we may find common ground with those of other faiths (or none at all) as we address the pressing problems of our age. Our goal is not to solve all problems everywhere; our goal is, rather, to become the kind of people who bring Christ's joy to the world as we build a human community based on God's justice and peace.

Chapter 6, "Prayer," looks at the foundation of our vocation, our relationship with the Lord. We need to stay close to God in prayer. The Benedictine practices of communal prayer through the Office and the individual prayer of *lectio divina* help us to deepen our relationship with God and thereby see where we are called to serve in our world.

This book is the product of many years of experience as a lay Catholic trying to live a unified life. It would not have been possible without the help of many people, only some of whom can be mentioned here. I want to acknowledge the many good people I have met over the years while volunteering in parishes, people who helped me see how our work was part of our call. Now, as a theology professor, I want to thank those parishioners who responded with enthusiasm and encouraged me to write this book. I would like to acknowledge the group who read these chapters as they were being prepared and gave me such helpful feedback and suggestions for improvements, especially Joy and Paul Fleckser, Melissa Walsh, Fr. Phillip Timko, Fr. James Flint, and Chad Suhr. I would also like to thank the monks of St. Procopius Abbey, especially Fr. Becket Franks, Fr. David Turner, and Fr. Julian von Duerbeck for formation in Benedictine spirituality. Finally, I would like to thank my husband, Peter, for his unstinting support and encouragement.

Christine M. Fletcher
Feast of St. Procopius 2014

chapter 1

Faith and Life

Many of us feel a separation between our religious life, when we pray or go to Mass, and our "normal" life. It is hard to see our work as part of God's call for us. It is even harder to see getting involved in politics or coaching the youth soccer team as something God is interested in. Speaking theologically we are experiencing the split between the church and the secular world. The church is the body of Christ, the people of God. At one and the same time it is participating in the kingdom of God and being present on earth. It is the heavenly kingdom beginning but not yet fully realized.

On the other hand we have the secular world where we work and live, pay a mortgage, raise our children, and try to get through the day. It seems to run on completely different rules from the church. For many people there is a huge gap between the church and the world, the church is for religious people and the world is for normal people. Religious people shouldn't bring their faith into their secular life; faith is okay as a private security blanket, but it must not challenge the way the world works. This is the dilemma that lay Christians face in trying to live a life of discipleship where every part of life is under the lordship of Christ.

Saint Thomas Aquinas pointed out that "world" has three meanings in Scripture. First, it signifies God's creation, and so the world is good (Gen 1:31). Second, it implies creation reaching perfection in Christ: "God was, in Christ, reconciling the world to himself" (2 Cor 5:19). If the world is reaching perfection in Christ it is because something is wrong with it. What is wrong with the world is the third meaning of "world" for St. Thomas—the world as creation marred by sin: "The whole world lies under the power of the evil one" (1 John 5:19).[1]

The Jewish and Christian creation story tells us that when God created the world, he created beings in his image, like God in some way. The writers of the ancient account in Genesis 2–3 tell us of Adam and Eve and how God gave them one law to obey, not to eat the fruit of the tree of knowledge of good and evil. These first humans had freedom to choose whether to obey God or use their freedom to seek their own will. They chose their own will, and that choice meant that the world no longer was in harmony with God's will but bound over to the power of the evil one. Relations between man and woman, humanity and nature, and those within nature now had difficulty, pain, and death. This is not a factual report of two people in a garden, but is a story that tells us a deeper truth: original sin affects all of creation. G. K. Chesterton said that the one empirically verifiable doctrine of the church was original sin. When we look around at our good intentions gone wrong, or when we try to change a bad habit and fail over and over, we realize the power of this original sin. *The Catechism of the Catholic Church* tells us that because of original sin, "human nature is weakened in its powers; subject to ignorance, suffering and the domination of death; and inclined to sin" (418). The world, which is good because it is God's creation, is disordered because of sin; it is corrupt and corrupting. The secular vocation of the laity in the world is to try to make God's love and justice real in a world marked by greed, selfishness, and sin. We believe we can do this because we have been reconciled to God through Jesus Christ's life, death, and resurrection. Our baptism makes us members of Christ's body the church, and so we are part of God's work of reconciliation.

Even though the divide between the church and the world as fallen creation seems pretty clear, we must find a way to bridge the gap and live our faith 24/7 in the world and in church. This requires us to change ourselves, the kind of people we are. Our choices form our character; if we choose goodness, we become good people. Our Christian life of the sacraments, our personal prayer, and our moral efforts with God's grace work together to make us the kind of people who can bring God's love to the world. We are also responsible for bringing God's love to each part of our lives: to change the world, to alleviate pain, to correct injustices, to care for others. We know we will never create a utopia here on earth but that doesn't excuse us. We must make our work, family, and community life part of building up God's kingdom on earth.

The early Christians lived like this. The time of the early church, the apostolic age, was a time when Rome was the center of a globalized economy, where there existed stock markets, commodity trading, sexual license of every description, abortion, and divorce. Slavery was common, and a man's wife and children were his property. It was a multiethnic, multireligion culture unified by Rome's political and administrative system. Christianity was one religious sect among many. Christians had a bad reputation: they were considered *atheists* because they denied the state gods and did not take part in emperor worship; *cannibals* because they spoke of the Eucharist as eating the flesh and blood of Christ; and *incestuous* because they called each other brother and sister. Christians usually couldn't go out and openly convert others, they had to rely on the witness of their lives.

Their neighbors would learn about Christianity from knowing them and how they behaved, or by attending the circuses where Christians were tortured and killed. Lucian wrote:

> You see, these misguided creatures start with the general conviction that they are immortal for all time, which explains the contempt of death and voluntary self-devotion which are so common among them; and then it was impressed on them by their original lawgiver that they are all brothers, from the moment that they are converted,

and deny the gods of Greece, and worship the crucified sage, and live after his laws. All this they take quite on trust, with the result that they despise all worldly goods alike, regarding them merely as common property.[2]

Christians were committed to their beliefs and knew why they mattered. Saint Paul wrote to the Christians in Corinth, "If Christ has not been raised, your faith is futile and you are still in your sins. Then those also who have died in Christ have perished. If for this life only we have hoped in Christ, we are of all people most to be pitied. But in fact Christ has been raised from the dead, the first fruits of those who have died" (1 Cor 15:17-20). Belief in the resurrection, which changes everything in life, was the power at the heart of the Christian message. Humanity was no longer the victim of cruel gods, condemned to a life filled with pain ending in death. For Christians life is changed not ended at death; knowing that enabled them to face persecution and torture with equanimity, and even joy. Lucian recognized their courage.

The Christians in those days were normal people; it wasn't a time of bliss with no dissension in the local churches. Most of the epistles show us communities where disputes and factions had arisen, and the normal human behavior of honoring the rich and despising the poor occurred. But in addition to this there was fervor, a joy from the Good News of Christ's resurrection that meant Christians were prepared to live in a new way. They took their place in society as far as they could and lived according to their faith.

When the church was accepted and Christianity became the state religion new problems arose, but the idea of the unity of faith and life permeated society. We can refer to these ages in Western Europe as Christendom. The church seemed to order all parts of society: politics, economics, war, and family life. Kings looked to the pope for support, and the church definitely thought it had the answers for many worldly concerns. This was the source of new problems, as historians of the church know. However, in daily life, the church ordered not just prayer on Sunday, but the round of days. In an age of serfdom, holy days offered a release from toil and a chance to rest and hopefully to feast.

In the Reformation, Christendom was divided, and religion became the cause for wars; it seemed that religion was the problem and not the solution. The ruler decided what religion the people were to follow. Obviously that didn't work, we have Protestant martyrs, Catholic martyrs, Anabaptist martyrs— all Christians condemned to death by other Christians for believing and worshiping differently from the state church. Religion seemed to be a hindrance to peace and civil order.

New scientific discoveries such as the Copernican system (the Galileo case) and evolution saw the churches and science seemingly opposed to one another. This was at least partly the effect of misguided clerics who read Scripture as if it were a science textbook. Then in the age of the Industrial Revolution, the churches seemed to be on the side of the owners, not the workers who endured such terrible conditions. Marx called religion the opiate of the masses. Christianity seemed not only out of date and ignorant, it seemed to be an oppressor of working people.

The Preconciliar Church

By the nineteenth century the church and the world were viewed as competitors. In the church, the "world became both the enemy to be feared and avoided, and at the same time the 'unchurched' were to be conquered for Christ."[3] The laity were seen to need protection from the depravities of the secular world. A Catholic culture of schools, hospitals, universities, pious confraternities and societies grew up, a kind of Catholic mirror of secular activities. In America, the Catholic experience was of an immigrant church needing to protect itself against a society predominately Anglo and Protestant.

The experience of worship divided the laity from the clergy. The experience which most Catholics had of the church's prayer, particularly the Eucharist, was one of praying alone in their native language while the priest—at the altar with his back to the congregation—was saying the Mass in Latin. This fostered a sense among the laity that we were the passive recipients within the church; the real church was the priest who was performing the sacraments and the religious who ran the schools and hospitals.

The ecclesial infrastructure of the nineteenth and early twentieth centuries produced a strong Catholic culture that was inward-looking and institutionally focused. It meant many Catholics could live without routinely interacting with unbelievers. In this Catholic culture, many believers saw their faith as requiring them to stay within the narrow sphere of parish and special spiritual work. Cardinal Joseph Suenens, who later would be one of the major figures of the Second Vatican Council, described this in a book he wrote in the 1950s, "In the eyes of too many 'practicing' Catholics, a Christian life is reduced, alas! to a few religious exercises: Sunday Mass, Easter Communion, abstinence on Friday; and observing some commandments, particularly the sixth, on which attention is concentrated, as if the duty of justice, for instance, were not as binding as that of chastity."[4]

Burying oneself in parochial and spiritual concerns is illustrated in a story of a priest's visit to very good Catholics, asking for their cooperation in reaching out to the unchurched. The father refused, "So you would like me to do your work for you?" The mother excused herself on principle, "It is a matter of principle with me, Father, not to interfere in what is not my business." The daughter, when told she would be wanting in charity if she did not help, responded, "I, wanting in charity! Oh! Father, how little you know me, I never interfere with anyone." Finally the younger brother, an ecclesiastical student at home for the holidays, when asked what he had been doing for souls, replied, "I have not had the opportunity." Suenens commented that there is a need to revise our Christian education since it produced such an inward-looking and narrow conception of discipleship.[5]

Reinforcing this culture was the understanding of the church as the "perfect society," governed by the hierarchy. In practice this meant that most lay Catholics identified the clergy as the church. Obedience was the prime virtue of the layperson. This caricature of Catholicism, of the docile laity taking their orders from the priests, was the basis of much of the anti-Catholic sentiment in America. It contributed to the common view that religion, any religion, is an unwelcome participant in the marketplace of ideas. Religion is supposed to be your private activity; not something that impacts how you work, vote, or spend your money.

This divide between secular life and the church may have been a consequence of these forces, but it is not correct theologically. It ignores what Suenens called the central paradox of our faith that "combines the prospect of life after death, which lifts us from the earth and makes us raise our eyes to heaven, with the lesson of the Incarnation, which teaches us to take upon ourselves in the sweat of our brow the immediate temporal happiness of men."[6] Christians are to care for and about the world they live in.

The Second Vatican Council and Today's World

The Second Vatican Council ushered in a new relationship between the church and the world. First of all, it recognized freedom of conscience, and it initiated many of the ecumenical and inter-religious dialogues that we take for granted today. Second, it gave us the conception of the church as the people of God, a pastoral and more egalitarian vision to correct the excesses of the "perfect society" model of church with the pope on top and the lay faithful at the bottom of the pyramid. Third, it called on the church to dialogue with the world, to read the signs of the times and engage with culture. Together this meant that Vatican II recognized the laity's role to order the world rightly, and our autonomy to do so as we have knowledge from living in the situation. This does not eliminate the challenge of living in a fallen world with a fallen human nature. The old temptations—the world, the flesh and the devil, the world and its goods, the desires of the flesh, and the demonic sin of pride—must be faced in a new environment.

Fortress Catholicism had withdrawn into a special Catholic world (where those old temptations were as strong as ever). Today we are encouraged to go into the world, learn the signs of the times, and see both the good and the bad. The world of the 1960s, the time of the council, certainly needed the witness of the church as it hovered on the brink of nuclear war. The peace movement became part of living the faith for some Catholics. Other Catholics were galvanized by the pro-life movement and got involved in politics. Many, disturbed by the coarsening of culture (particularly movies and television) to increased violence and ever-more explicit sexual depictions, wanted to retreat to a safer Christian world.

Today our challenge is living the faith in an interconnected virtual world that annihilates time and space. Our contemporary world can simultaneously bring us together in a global community and isolate us in our own private virtual reality. We are in touch with people around the globe, but on our terms. Every idea is on offer; we have a spiritual buffet where practices from the world's different religions are presented as of equal interest or worth. People who are repelled by the idea of an all-knowing benevolent God watching over their lives find themselves instead living under the watchful eyes of speed cameras, GPS locators, and the NSA. Like all human inventions, the wired world brings us challenges and gifts. Like any new technology, we have to learn to humanize it and decide how it fits into a truly human life. While pornography is one of the big businesses of the Internet, many Christians have embraced the new technology and use it as a way to witness to God's love and care for everyone, promoting justice and peace.

Our technological advances have meant that more people are facing not the problems of starvation and subsistence living (though too many people still do face these), but the problem of handling wealth. Christians throughout history faced the temptation of making wealth into an idol. The church has always warned us of the temptations of worldly goods. There are two deadly sins directly related to wealth and possessions: gluttony and avarice. Envy and pride are also related to wealth, but more to what it buys in terms of power or status. We are warned about misuse of wealth in the gospels, by early church fathers such as St. Basil and St. John Chrysostom, and in the great writers of the Middle Ages, Chaucer and Dante. These warnings were written in a society with a small-scale economy where markets were between buyers and sellers who knew each other and would have to trade with one another in an ongoing relationship. Goods were limited by the technology of production. Scarcity of food, clothing, and other necessities was a fact of life for most.

That has all changed drastically. The advances of human creativity and productivity mean that the poorest people in America today live better than the lords of medieval Europe. Clothing is now something we can buy as a disposable good instead of something to be cared for and, when possible, reused. Food is plentiful and relatively cheap. Most people, even those on low incomes, have a television. If wealth was a challenge in a society where most people experienced scarcity, it is an even greater challenge in our society. We have advanced in technology and wealth, but we have not changed our fundamentally flawed human nature. We know that we have always had a problem with our desires, we want more of everything. In an era of mass production, those out-of-control desires meet advertising designed to stimulate them. The result is consumerism.

Our world is marked by an unconscious acceptance, by Christians as much as everyone else, of a consumerist worldview that is opposed to gospel values. Our generally accepted measure of prosperity, the Gross National Product (GNP), is based on mass consumption. The mass consumption is encouraged by marketing and advertising that is ever present. Baptist theologian Harvey Cox has described consumerism as a religion in "The Market Is My Shepherd, and I Shall Want and Want and Want."[7]

Consumerism has unstated assumptions about human beings, the purpose of life and its components, the economy, society, and the state, which are vastly different from those in the Gospel. In the gospel story, people have inherent worth, whether they are young or old, sick or healthy, fit or unfit. They are designed for a community life that stewards and protects the gifts of nature. There are things that are of so much value they should not be sold. In the consumerist narrative, however, people are autonomous individuals, valued for being young, healthy, fit, and wealthy. Everything can be sold, nature is just something to be used, and the only purpose of life is to buy more stuff to keep the economy growing. This makes us blind to the real values of the world that God made for all his creatures. Pope Francis feels this: "How many of us, myself included, have lost our bearings; we are no longer attentive to the world in which we live; we don't care; we don't protect what God created for everyone, and we end up unable even to care for one another!"[8]

Solving the very real problems of this world is the way laypeople today live their call to follow God. As laity in the world, we have to figure out for ourselves how to change a world in a culture that doesn't pretend to be based on God's law. It says instead that a good life is immediate pleasure and infinite choice. Most people in the world, even in the business and the advertising agencies and marketing departments, want to live a good life that is full of purpose, but find little help in learning how to do so. Our religious discussions tend to focus on individual spirituality and morality rather than on witnessing to the world at large.

The council fathers tell us that God's way of love "is not something reserved for important matters, but must be exercised above all in the ordinary circumstances of daily life" (*Gaudium et Spes* 38). We must live the way Christ taught us and bring all parts of life—our ownership of goods, our marriages, and our freedom—to reflect this way of love. We need to bring this way of love to places where the priests and religious are not usually found: our homes, our offices, Wall Street, Main Street, the mall, the PTA meeting, the Little League field, and the senior center.

We are like the early Christians. We will be witnessing in a world of people who believe in many religions or in none. Our witness must begin a dialogue that respects others as persons and believers. Lately, it is those of no professed faith who have been calling us to live up to our faith. The sustainability movement warns us that we are using up the earth's resources in our wasteful consumer lifestyle, polluting the air and water, and depriving future generations of their rights in this world. The so-called "New Atheists" criticize us for not doing anything about the very real problems that exist in our world, but going along with the dominant culture. They see us using religion as a cosmic security blanket.

Our task is both more urgent and more difficult because of the clerical sex abuse scandals. Those who do not wish to listen to any church teaching just bring up the sex scandals and tune out. We must acknowledge the evil that was done and pray for healing of the victims and the church. But we cannot let this scandal, or anything else, stop us from witnessing to Christ and his love for us, sinners though we are.

Each of us is called to be a disciple, and each of us has a special mission. We are prepared for it by the uniqueness of our identity: our gifts and talents, our personality, the time and place we were born. We have a specific situation in which to use our gifts and specific challenges to answer. To prepare for this great work and to understand what being a disciple of Jesus means, we start with Sacred Scripture—especially the Gospels, the record of Jesus in the world. That is the topic of the following chapter.

chapter 2

God Calls Us in Scripture

To understand our vocation as Christians, we start with Scripture. This chapter provides a short introduction to Scripture in relation to vocation. It can only be a very short introduction, but it should yield several tools to continue reading and praying with the Bible on your own, or perhaps in a Bible study or small faith-sharing group. The chapter begins by describing how Catholics read and pray with Scripture. The church gave us the Scriptures, and it helps us understand them. We don't read them as if God dictated them word for word, and we don't use the Scriptures as if we can read any one verse in isolation. We won't find a message, "Chris, be a shepherd"; instead we will build a relationship with God, enabling ourselves to hear God speak to us.

Then we turn to the Gospel of Mark, a gospel of discipleship, where we will do two exercises: first, read through the entire Gospel of Mark in one sitting and, second, put that gospel back into Peter's voice as he preached and taught. We look at the structure of the gospel, and what it tells us about our call to holiness, the call all Christians share—priests and people alike.

Next we look at some selected passages to see how Christ called ordinary people to be his disciples. We know our call is to holiness, to forming our lives on the gospel story, but what is my particular call? Reading the gospels and paying attention to the extras, the crowd, and to several of the walk-on characters illustrate several key points: everyone is called, and no one is outside God's love; not everyone is called to the special work of church ministry; and, finally, those called to live in the world have special difficulties to overcome. The largest difficulty, as we have seen, is wealth, so the chapter concludes by looking at some of the rich people in the gospel and some parables that speak about how to handle wealth.

Reading Scripture as a Catholic

Our call from God is the call to be like him. In baptism we are made children of God, the Holy Spirit comes to dwell within us. God has made us holy through this sacrament, and the purpose of our life is to become more and more God-like. Irenaeus put it like this: "The Word of God, our Lord Jesus Christ, who did, through His transcendent love, become what we are, that He might bring us to be even what He is Himself."[1] To know more about Jesus we need to read the gospels that tell us his birth, life, teachings, death, and resurrection. We need to fit our life story to the gospel story.

The Bible is a difficult book to approach without help, because it is actually a library, not a single book. It does have a single plotline, God's love for his creation, but it is a story told in various types of books: history, prophecy, poetry, and letters. The Bible has a simple theme: God loves us more than we can imagine. The plotline is the story of God's purpose for us—an easy way to remember it is C4E: Creation, Covenant, Christ, Church, and End Times. At the *creation* of the world we are made in the image of God, when we used our freedom to please ourselves instead of to serve God, that is, when we sinned. Humanity rejected God, and God responds to human disobedience with a promise his plan of love will be fulfilled, the *covenant*. He chooses Israel for his own, and in the fullness of time sends his own Son, Jesus the *Christ*, to reconcile humanity and God through his life, death, and resurrection. The *church* is Christ's body on earth until the *end of time,* the new creation when all is made well.

The Old Testament tells Israel's story from the prehistory of Genesis through the postexilic prophets. In between are works of history such as the books of Kings and Samuel; works of poetry, such as the Psalms; and books of prophecy. The New Testament begins with the appearance of Jesus. His life and works, death and resurrection are covered in the four gospels. The Acts of the Apostles tell us of the early days of the church and the missionary journeys of St. Paul. The epistles or letters of Paul, Peter, James, Jude, and John follow. These were letters to the young Christian communities, teaching them the faith, dealing with disturbances in the groups of believers, and answering their questions. Finally, we have the book of Revelation, a book about the end of time, the passing away of all we know and the coming of the new heaven and new earth. You can see that these different books must be read in different ways. Often people read all of the Bible as if it were a newspaper — so you have people reading Genesis as if it were a science textbook and Revelation as if it were the playbook for exactly how God is going to punish sinners! Catholics don't read the Bible like that.

When we read the Bible we read with the mind of the church. It is a team effort and not an individual one. We should follow the criteria for interpreting Scripture that the fathers of the Second Vatican Council gave us:

1. be attentive to "the content and unity of the whole of Scripture";
2. read Scripture within the living tradition "of the entire church"; and
3. be attentive to the analogy of faith (the way the faith as revealed all fits together. (*Dei Verbum* 12; see also *Catechism of the Catholic Church* [hereafter CCC] 112–14).

The "whole faith" includes four things:
1. what we believe, the Creed;
2. how we worship, the sacraments;
3. how we live, the Ten Commandments and the Beatitudes; and
4. how we pray, the Our Father.

If we read Scripture this way, we may be puzzled at times, but we won't make the mistake of reading one verse out of context. In other words, we won't find ourselves handling poisonous snakes or drinking poison because Mark 16:18 says, "They will pick up snakes in their hands, and if they drink any deadly thing, it will not hurt them; they will lay their hands on the sick, and they will recover."

Scripture provides us a guide to God's purpose for creation as a whole, and for each of us as individuals. The purpose of the creation and our own purpose are related. Both creation stories start with God making: "In the beginning when God created" (Gen 1:1), and "In the day that the Lord God made the earth and the heavens" (Gen 2:4). What is particularly relevant to us is that we are made in the image of God: "Then God said, 'Let us make humankind in our image, according to our likeness; . . . So God created humankind in his image, in the image of God he created them; male and female he created them'" (Gen 1:26-27). Dorothy L. Sayers, an English mystery writer and lay theologian, saw it this way: "It is observable that in the passage leading up to the statement about man, he [the author] has given no detailed information about God. Looking at man, he sees in him something essentially divine, but when we turn back to see what he says about the original upon which the 'image' of God was modeled, we find only the single assertion, 'God created.' The characteristic common to God and man is apparently that: the desire and the ability to make things."[2] Our activity in the world, our ability to create paintings and chocolate cakes and especially our gift of procreating children, is an image of the loving God creating out of love.

The fathers of the Second Vatican Council further explain the image of God in humans: "Man was created in God's image and was commanded to conquer the earth with all it contains and to rule the world in justice and holiness" (GS 34); "All it contains" includes our family life, our communities, and definitely our human work. The Scriptures tell us of doctors and farmers, scholars, sailors and builders, housewives, shepherds, merchants, servants and slaves. The Bible shows us an agrarian society with roles assigned by gender and birth. Priesthood came along with membership in the tribe of Levi, for example. When we get to the New Testament we have the same agrarian world in the background, but we also have the power of Rome and its armies, its governing officials, and an urban culture in Rome and Jerusalem.

In the gospels we read the account of God himself made human, Jesus Christ, active in the world. He was part of the established religion of Israel; he was subject to the political rule of the Roman Empire and their puppet princes in Palestine. From St. Joseph he learned a trade, carpentry, at which he worked until he began his ministry. The four gospels give us accounts that aren't exactly the same but show us what happens when God becomes man: the lame walk, the blind see, water turns into wine, and the only truly innocent man in the history of the world is executed for disturbing society. But the story doesn't end there. The resurrection of Christ means that death's power is broken; from that time forward death means life is *changed*, not ended.

Since Jesus lived a human life, and the gospel writers recorded incidents from it for us, we can read the gospels and see what kind of world God meant this to be, and what kind of people we are meant to be. Disciples try to be like their master. When we read and pray with the gospels we pay attention to Christ interacting with all kinds of people—eating and drinking, fasting and praying, teaching and healing. Reading and meditating on the gospels will help us understand how we are called by God to holiness, to a state in life, and to particular work and relationships. The Bible is the living word of God; when we read it with prayerful hearts and open minds we allow God to speak to us. The gospels form the heart, the source of our actions and attitudes. The practice of praying the Bible the Benedictine way is detailed in chapter 6.

The Gospel of Mark

The Gospel of Mark is called the gospel of discipleship; its author has three main points for his readers: (1) Who is Christ? The Son of God. (2) How do we follow him? Be a disciple. (3) What does being a disciple mean? It means following Christ to the cross, giving up our self-will, loving others, and bearing suffering and hardships patiently. This is the good news we don't want to hear.

The gospel is vivid and realistic: "Mark writes about Jesus with a great human realism that Matthew and Luke often omit or tone down."[3] Mark is called a gospel of discipleship, yet it is a story of disciples who repeatedly failed their master. They lived with Jesus and were blind to his identity; they saw the miracles, gathered up the baskets of leftovers after Christ fed the crowd with five loaves and two fish, and still didn't understand. They ran away from him and denied him when he got in trouble with the authorities. Even the faithful women, who followed Jesus through the gospel and stayed by the cross when the others were hiding, failed at the end, being so afraid of the idea of the resurrection that the gospel says: "So they went out and fled from the tomb, for terror and amazement had seized them; and they said nothing to anyone, for they were afraid" (Mark 16:8).

This gospel of human failure was actually a gospel of great hope to its first audience. Mark was writing to a church undergoing persecution. His first readers knew that Peter, who failed so often, became the rock who strengthened his brothers. This taught them that their failures are not the last word. Today we can read Mark and recognize ourselves in the blind, fearful disciples. They were saved and transformed, and we can be too.

Exercise 1

Read the Gospel of Mark from beginning to end in a single sitting. See how the plot develops and the story reaches its climax. Reading the whole gospel as a single work should give you a sense of how the gospel writer saw the events unfold as a whole revelation from God.

The Universal Call to Holiness

If you have done the exercise above, my guess is that you were astonished at how quickly the story moved from the early days in Galilee through the journey to Jerusalem to the culmination in the Last Supper, the trial, crucifixion, burial, and resurrection of Jesus.

Mark wastes no time but confronts us with the central paradox of our faith: the criminal on the cross is the picture and model of how we are to love. By his love for the Father and for us and by his willing obedience, Jesus reconciled sinners to God. He let evil do its worst to him, bearing it in love for us. This is the story we need to follow in our lives. We need to recognize ourselves as sinners who need God's mercy and forgiveness. We need to love and forgive others.

How this plays out in our lives is simple to say but hard to do. In Mark 9, Jesus tells his disciples about his coming passion and death, but they don't understand him. As they walk together, an argument breaks out among them about who is going to be the greatest. Jesus gives them his way: "Whoever wants to be first must be last of all and servant of all" (Mark 9:35). So not only are they following a leader who predicts that the political powers will arrest and kill him; he will love and serve and let this happen. Not only that, he expects his disciples to do the same: to be humble and be servants. It is a consistent but unwelcome message to them and to us.

In Mark 12, Jesus is being challenged by the religious and political establishment. A scribe who has heard the others disputing with Jesus asks what is the greatest commandment. "Jesus answered, 'The first is, "Hear, O Israel: the Lord our God, the Lord is one; you shall love the Lord your God with all your heart, and with all your soul, and with all your mind, and with all your strength." The second is this, "You shall love your neighbor as yourself." There is no other commandment greater than these' " (Mark 12:29-31).

This is the same call we heard in Mark 9—to be a servant to both God and neighbor. This is the universal call to holiness reduced to the bare essentials. Here is all the morality in Scripture from the Ten Commandments and the Beatitudes. We talk about the commandments as two tablets: the first tablet is about loving God—have no other Gods, don't take God's name in vain, and worship God alone—and the second tablet is about loving our neighbor—honor your parents, don't kill, don't steal, don't lie, moderate your desires for sex, power, and wealth. It's all very clear. If we are honest, however, none of us can keep these commandments. We fail again and again. If we don't recognize that fact, the gospel will never be good news to us, because the good news is that we are loved even as we fail. When we fail we can take heart from Peter, who failed, but always asked forgiveness and kept trying. That is the model of discipleship we need. To see this more clearly, try exercise 2.

Exercise 2

Tradition tells us that this gospel was written by Mark, a companion of Peter. Gerald O'Mahony, SJ, "decided to experiment and turned the whole of the Gospel of Mark back into the way Peter would have told it in the first person. . . . Not only did it work like a dream, but the Gospel came alive for me as I wrote it out word by word and verse by verse."[4] So Fr. O'Mahony would read Mark 1:16-18 like this: "And passing along by the Sea of Galilee, he saw me and Andrew my brother casting a net in the sea; for we were fishermen. And Jesus said to us, 'Follow me and I will make you fishers of men.' And immediately we left our nets and followed him."

Rewriting the gospel as if we were Peter shows us how Peter has owned up to every mistake he made, nothing was held back. It makes the words that we hear in church come alive. When we put ourselves in Peter's place we see this gospel is a story of hope for everyone who knows just how often they mess things up. Perfect people do not fit here, but sinners are always welcome.

As Fr. O'Mahony suggests, work your way through the Gospel of Mark, experiencing it through Peter's eyes.

The Extras and the Walk-ons

So far we have seen how the whole gospel proclaims the universal call to holiness. This call to become more like Christ is given to every Christian in baptism. Within that call we as individuals have particular vocations. We are born to a family in a particular place and a particular time. We have inborn tendencies and talents. Each of us has some work in building up the kingdom of God, and most of us are not called to become priests or religious.

We are accustomed to the gospel writers' focus on Jesus and his close disciples. Doing the exercise above makes plain why the gospel is written as it is—Peter was telling Mark the important things that happened. Every Sunday we listen to a passage at Mass and we naturally focus on Jesus, as we should. We need to ponder all of his actions and sayings and apply them to our life today. These teachings are essential to living our call to holiness.

But we who work in the world can sometimes feel that the gospel is not talking directly to us, but only to those in church leadership. It seems that to be a truly committed Christian, we need to have some official role of ministry. To correct this perspective, it is helpful to read the gospels as if they are movies. First, we have the main characters: Jesus and the apostles (the good guys) on the one hand and the Romans, the Pharisees, and the Sadducees (the baddies) on the other. The interaction between them drives the story. But movies have extras and walk-on characters too. Their lives are a mystery to us—we see them appear, interact with the main characters, and leave, and in so doing they move the story forward. Looking at the extras and walk-ons as we read the gospels enables us to see our own call as lay Christians. If we look at both the extras (the crowd that often appears in the gospels) and the walk-ons (those whom Jesus called directly), we see that we all are called to take up the cross, and each of us is called to live and work and love God in our own particular situation.

The Extras—The Crowd

At the beginning of his gospel, Mark recounts how one evening when Jesus was in Peter's house the crowd came to see Jesus, who healed them. The narrative rushes us along to the next incident, but it's helpful to ask: Who were those people and what happened to them? It would be safe to say that some in the crowd wanted to see the latest thing, the celebrity of Galilee. Others were looking for someone to trust in, someone to tell them about God. Some of them probably found belief in God almost natural, others a constant struggle. All of them probably told others about what they saw, just like we discuss the latest event in our lives.

The crowds come to hear Jesus teach, have him heal their sick, and get food. Imagine being part of the crowd who were so eager to hear Jesus that when they saw where his boat was heading they ran to that place. Jesus takes pity on them, teaches them, feeds them miraculously with five loaves and two fish (Mark 6:30-45), and then dismisses them. Put yourself in the place of someone in that crowd. You have given up a day's wage to find and hear Jesus. You eat the bread of this miracle. Mark doesn't tell us what Jesus' dismissal to the crowd was, but based on other stories in the gospel, "Go and sin no more" or "See how God cares for you" might be good guesses. How would you feel going back to daily life? Wouldn't you tell your friends about that amazing day? Wouldn't you try to remember everything Jesus said, and do it?

It is from the crowd that Jesus selects his special followers, the twelve apostles. Not being one of the Twelve doesn't mean that we aren't called to be witnesses to our faith. We are included in the call to follow to the cross: "He called the *crowd* [emphasis added] with his disciples, and said to them, 'If any want to become my followers, let them deny themselves and take up their cross and follow me. For those who want to save their life will lose it, and those who lose their life for my sake, and for the sake of the gospel, will save it'" (Mark 8:34-35).

People then were just as unwilling to suffer hardships as we are today. This was a hard teaching. We know the crowd in the New Testament was fickle; they cried "Hosanna!" on Palm Sunday, and "Crucify him!" on Good Friday. It is a reminder for us that we need to have the virtue of faith—to stick to our beliefs and not be swayed by the latest fad or discouraged at hardships.

After Jesus' resurrection and ascension, a crowd assembled again in Jerusalem for Pentecost. Out of that crowd three thousand people who had heard Peter preaching were converted and baptized. I often wonder how many of that crowd had been part of the crowd that was fed with the five loaves, or maybe they were someone who had seen Jesus teaching or healing. Whatever their background, that day they became witnesses who carried this story of Jesus and his resurrection across the empire, preparing the way for the apostles. Most of them continued to live their normal lives—but in a new way.

The Walk-Ons

In addition to the extras, the crowds, the gospels have walk-on characters. We know them by name or by description. They come to Jesus, have a significant interaction with him, and then disappear. As we meditate on Scripture, these characters can help us discover how to follow Jesus in everyday life. I have chosen some examples of people who came to Jesus and were sent back to their normal lives, unlike Peter, Matthew, and the others who were called out of their normal lives to become apostles.

In the first chapter of Mark, where all the exciting things pile one on top of another, we see Jesus come to the house of Simon and Andrew. "As soon as they left the synagogue, they entered the house of Simon and Andrew, with James and John. Now Simon's mother-in-law was in bed with a fever, and they told him about her at once. He came and took her by the hand and lifted her up. Then the fever left her, and she began to serve them" (Mark 1:29-31). That is the last we hear of her, but she embodies everything we need to know about our life and vocation. We need the Lord to heal us, and when he does we must serve others in our life. She did it by helping with the dinner—her job in her time and her place. Our call is just as immediate every day.

All followers of Jesus, not just the apostles or those called to ministry, should be bringing others to him. When we find the Lord, and realize how much he loves us and everyone else, we should be anxious to share that good news with others. We can see an example of this kind of faith in the story of the healing of the paralytic (Mark 2:1-12). A paralyzed man is lowered through the roof by his friends because they cannot get him to Jesus through the crowd. Mark focuses our attention on the interchange between Jesus and the Pharisees, which sets up an opposition between Jesus and the religious establishment (eventually culminating in the crucifixion). Within that episode, though, is another story, a story of great faith of the friends and of the paralyzed man. The paralytic allows himself to be carried to Jesus, trusting his friends not to drop him when they decide that the only way to get through the crowd is to lower him through the roof. The friends were so convinced that Jesus could help that they took a risk of extreme action. Jesus commanded the paralytic to pick up his mat and go home. Saint Ambrose comments on this passage: "It was our Lord's custom to require of those whom he healed some response or duty to be done."[5]

The man's friends had already taken action based on faith in Jesus. One may surmise that in the excitement of seeing their friend healed, they ran downstairs to meet him. And perhaps they also repaired the roof. Presumably they all went back to their normal lives, but it is reasonable to think they were confirmed as believers in Jesus—maybe not as the Messiah at that point, but at least as someone who spoke for God, a prophet. After such an act of faith, surely they would have spoken about this incident to anyone they met.

Two outstanding examples of those who have a transforming encounter with Jesus and are sent back to their normal lives are two outsiders: the Gerasene demoniac and the Syrophoenician woman. They are important for us because they highlight how the Good News is for everyone. We don't get to exclude people from God's love and care.

The Gerasene demoniac lived in Gentile territory, and he was so possessed by evil spirits that chains could not hold him. Like the others possessed by demons in Mark, the man cries out Jesus' identity: "Jesus, Son of the Most High God" (Mark 5:7). When the man is healed and his neighbors come to see this miracle, they ask Jesus to leave: better to have a wild man in the neighborhood than someone with the power to heal him![6] The cured man asks to come with Jesus but is told, " 'Go home to your friends, and tell them how much the Lord has done for you, and what mercy he has shown you.' And he went away and began to proclaim in the Decapolis how much Jesus had done for him; and everyone was amazed" (Mark 5:19-20). The healed man is given his mission to his own people. He didn't need any more time in close contact with Jesus: he had already identified Jesus, the Son of the Most High God, and had been healed. He was ready to be a witness.

Jesus sends the healed demoniac to his own people. This could be a hard job; even Jesus had trouble in his home town of Nazareth (Mark 6:4-6). Generally speaking, if you want people to listen to a new idea, you need someone from out of town with a briefcase to present it. We don't respect the opinions of people we see every day as much as we do those of an outside expert. But this man had to go home. I am sure some people in his hometown didn't trust that he was truly healed; he would have met with some belief and with some rejection. But his mission is crystal clear: tell them what Jesus has done for you.

The Syrophoenician woman is doubly an outsider—a Gentile and a woman. She comes to Jesus when he is in the region of Tyre and Sidon, a region of historic enemies of the Jews. She and Jesus have an exchange where she gets the better of him: "She begged him to cast the demon out of her daughter. He said to her, 'Let the children be fed first, for it is not fair to take the children's food and throw it to the dogs.' But she answered him, 'Sir, even the dogs under the table eat the children's crumbs.' Then he said to her, 'For saying that, you may go—the demon has left your daughter.' So she went home, found the child lying on the bed, and the demon gone" (Mark 7:26-30).

This is the only place in the gospels where Jesus is bested in repartee.[7] This is a story of persistence, but also a gospel that shows us a human Jesus. Surely he was laughing, or at least smiling at her wit. And notice the woman's humility. She doesn't dispute that she is not one of the chosen, but she still has great faith in him. She leaves the gospel as suddenly as she entered. When we think about the story, however, it tells us that Jesus' fame had reached territory outside Galilee—those in the crowds who had followed Jesus had told their neighbors and friends about him. She wasn't Jewish, so she had heard about him in the talk among those whom she had met, probably in the marketplace. She heard enough to risk coming to meet him, making her request, and sticking around even when she meets with a harsh rejection. When Jesus promises her that her daughter is healed, she trusted Jesus' word and left. We don't have any evidence that she did anything but return to her normal life. But surely she told her neighbors what Jesus had done for her and repeatedly thanked God as she saw her daughter healthy and growing. If she did so, she prepared the way for the Gentile converts of the early church.

These walk-ons had some good news to share with others. This is the first obligation of being a disciple—telling others about Jesus by our lives and our words. We are called to do this in our own particular time and place, even in our secular work. Even work that may on the surface seem sinful can be accepted, as seen in this passage from Luke where John the Baptist is preaching to the crowd: "And the crowds asked him, 'What then should we do?' In reply [John] said to them, 'Whoever has two coats must share with anyone who has none; and whoever has food must do likewise.' Even tax collectors came to be baptized, and they asked him, 'Teacher, what should we do?' He said to them, 'Collect no more than the amount prescribed for you.' Soldiers also asked him, 'And we, what should we do?' He said to them, 'Do not extort money from anyone by threats or false accusation, and be satisfied with your wages'" (Luke 3:10-14).

Luke mentions soldiers and tax collectors specifically, because these are the visible face of the oppression of Israel by Rome. The soldiers are directly linked to the Roman government; the tax collectors are local Jews who collect the money for the occupying power. Both are despised by the local population. Both have the power to make peoples' lives miserable. John, God's prophet who prepares the way for Jesus, doesn't reject them. He doesn't ask soldiers to leave the army or the tax collectors to give up their day job. But he does require honesty, fair dealing, and care of the poor. He tells them to do their job honestly and for the good of all.

Jesus also has significant encounters with soldiers and tax collectors. Early in his ministry, Jesus is amazed by the centurion who asked that Jesus heal his servant not by coming and laying on hands but just by saying the word (Matt 8:5-13). At Jesus' death, it is a centurion in charge of the crucifixion, who says, "Truly this man was the Son of God" (Mark 15:39). The outsiders and oppressors have a better understanding of Jesus than many of his own people.

The tax collectors appear often. Early in Mark's gospel, Jesus calls Matthew (also called Levi) from his tax office. Matthew immediately follows and hosts a dinner at his house for the Lord. Matthew invited his friends, the tax collectors and sinners. Jesus eats with them and is criticized by the Pharisees, the religious leaders of the Jews, for doing so. But Jesus replies that, just as it is the sick who need a physician, he has come not to call the righteous but sinners (Mark 3:14-17). Jesus called Matthew to be an apostle. There is a different call for Zacchaeus, the tax collector who was so short he had to climb a tree to see Jesus. Jesus tells him to come down and host him for dinner!

All the people saw this and began to mutter, "He has gone to be the guest of a sinner."

But Zacchaeus stood up and said to the Lord, "Look, Lord! Here and now I give half of my possessions to the poor, and if I have cheated anybody out of anything, I will pay back four times the amount."

Jesus said to him, "Today salvation has come to this house, because this man, too, is a son of Abraham. For the Son of Man came to seek and to save the lost" (Luke 19:1-10). There is no suggestion here that Zacchaeus needed a new job; he just needed to care for the poor, do his job fairly, and make restitution for the times he had cheated. By keeping Zacchaeus in his job, the Lord lightened the tax burden on the whole city (no more kickbacks for Zacchaeus) and so helped the whole society, especially the poor. Zacchaeus's story contrasts strongly with that of the person we call the rich young man:

> As he was setting out on a journey, a man ran up and knelt before him, and asked him, "Good Teacher, what must I do to inherit eternal life?" Jesus said to him, "Why do you call me good? No one is good but God alone. You know the commandments: 'You shall not murder; You shall not commit adultery; You shall not steal; You shall not bear false witness; You shall not defraud; Honor your father and mother.'" He said to him, "Teacher, I have kept all these since my youth." Jesus, looking at him, loved him and said, "You lack one thing; go, sell what you own, and give the money to the poor, and you will have treasure in heaven; then come, follow me." When he heard this, he was shocked and went away grieving, for he had many possessions. (Mark 10:17-31)

Unlike Zacchaeus who was rich but not owned by his possessions, the rich young man showed that his wealth owned him. The rich young man seems to be someone who is living a moral life, he claims to have kept the commandments. But he can't face giving up his wealth. I think he wanted the security that wealth gives, rather than simply the wealth. He had made riches into his God. But Jesus was calling him to radical discipleship, and he was not prepared to trust Jesus and rely on God for everything in his life. He, like every human being, is in that situation every day. Our difficulties with wealth begin when we think we own things instead of remembering that everything is a gift from God and that we are only temporary administrators, or stewards. God gives us goods so that all humanity can live and no one goes hungry, naked, or homeless.

Wealth, Poverty, and Discipleship

Jesus calls all of us to remember that all are dependent on God and therefore we must care for each other but especially for those who are poor. This call cannot be ignored, it is central to discipleship, and it will cause us many difficulties. It goes against the ideas and spirit of our age, where success is defined by wealth and money can buy isolation in gated communities and private schools.

The divide between the rich and poor has been a problem since the beginning of time. The law of Moses provides for a jubilee year every forty-nine years to rebalance society and give everyone a fresh start. In the jubilee year debts were forgiven, bond-servanthood ended, and the members of each tribe regained their land, which they may have mortgaged or sold to others. The law was needed because during the forty nine years some grew richer and others poorer. Clearly God intends that all should have enough to survive and that extreme differences in wealth should be rebalanced. The idea of the jubilee reinforces the idea that all is gift and we are the stewards and caretakers of that gift.

Living as we do in a fallen world, there will be people who suffer, whose harvests fail or are destroyed, and widows and orphans. The prophets chastised Israel for neglecting the poor, the widows, and the orphans. In the psalms we read:

> Do not be afraid when some become rich,
>> when the wealth of their houses increases.
> For when they die they will carry nothing away;
>> their wealth will not go down after them. (Ps 49:16-17)

Or in our language, "you can't take it with you."

Again and again in the New Testament Jesus tells us how to handle our wealth. His most pointed teaching occurs in the prophecy of the Last Judgment, the sheep and the goats, in Matthew 25. Jesus tells us how we will be judged: Did we feed the hungry, cloth the naked, give drink to the thirsty, welcome the stranger, care for the sick, and visit the imprisoned? If we did this for the people we meet, then we have done it for him and will be welcomed into the kingdom. The instructions are very clear.

Mark's gospel did not include this parable but he does have others that are addressed precisely to our relationship with our goods. Two parables about sowing teach us the complexity of our relationship with wealth. The first, known as the parable of the sower, comes in two parts: the story told to the crowd and Jesus' explanation to the disciples:

> Again he began to teach beside the sea. Such a very large crowd gathered around him that he got into a boat on the sea and sat there, while the whole crowd was beside the sea on the land. He began to teach them many things in parables, and in his teaching he said to them: "Listen! A sower went out to sow. And as he sowed, some seed fell on the path, and the birds came and ate it up. Other seed fell on rocky ground, where it did not have much soil, and it sprang up quickly, since it had no depth of soil. And when the sun rose, it was scorched; and since it had no root, it withered away. Other seed fell among thorns, and the thorns grew up and choked it, and it yielded no grain. Other seed fell into good soil and brought forth grain, growing up and increasing and yielding thirty and sixty and a hundredfold." And he said, "Let anyone with ears to hear listen!"
> . . .
> The sower sows the word. These are the ones on the path where the word is sown: when they hear, Satan immediately comes and takes away the word that is sown in them. And these are the ones sown on rocky ground: when they hear the word, they immediately receive it with joy. But they have no root, and endure only for a while; then, when trouble or persecution arises on account of the word, immediately they fall away. And others are those sown among the thorns: these are the ones who hear the word, but the cares of the world, and the lure of wealth, and the desire for other things come in and

choke the word, and it yields nothing. And these are the ones sown on the good soil: they hear the word and accept it and bear fruit, thirty and sixty and a hundredfold. (Mark 4:1-9, 14-20)

This parable applies to all Christians. We can place ourselves in any one of the four places: at times our hearts are so hard that the seed is eaten up before it could take root; other times we rejoice at the message but then become discouraged. All of us experience the choking cares of daily life, the pressures on our time so that prayer or caring for others is neglected. But we also have times when we do hear and accept the word and bear fruit—although most times we are unaware of it because we are actually thinking about loving others.

As the parable of the sower highlights our response to God's word, a second parable about sowing shows us God's side: "He also said, 'The kingdom is as if someone would scatter seed on the ground, and would sleep and rise night and day, and the seed would sprout and grow, he does not know how. The earth produces of itself, first the stalk, then the head, then the full grain in the head. But when the grain is ripe, at once he goes in with his sickle, because the harvest has come'" (Mark 4:26-29).

The two parables read together paint a fuller picture of disciple-ship. The parable of the sower shows us the variety of human responses to God's love, and the parable of the seed's growth reminds us that all comes from God. Whatever goods we have are God's gift to us and are intended for the good of all. We cannot claim things are exclusively ours; we need to see our goods as given to us with a responsibility laid on us to use them wisely.

The parable of the wicked tenants drives home this point that all is gift, we own nothing but owe the Lord everything.

Then he began to speak to them in parables. "A man planted a vine-yard, put a fence around it, dug a pit for the wine press, and built a watchtower; then he leased it to tenants and went to another coun-try. When the season came, he sent a slave to the tenants to collect from them his share of the produce of the vineyard. But they seized him, and beat him, and sent him away empty-handed. And again he sent another slave to them; this one they beat over the head and

insulted. Then he sent another, and that one they killed. And so
it was with many others; some they beat, and others they killed.
He had still one other, a beloved son. Finally he sent him to them,
saying, 'They will respect my son.' But those tenants said to one
another, 'This is the heir; come, let us kill him, and the inheritance
will be ours.' So they seized him, killed him, and threw him out of
the vineyard. What then will the owner of the vineyard do? He will
come and destroy the tenants and give the vineyard to others. Have
you not read this scripture:
> 'The stone that the builders rejected
>   has become the cornerstone;
> this was the Lord's doing,
>   and it is amazing in our eyes'?"

When they realized that he had told this parable against them, they
wanted to arrest him, but they feared the crowd. So they left him
and went away. (Mark 12:1-12)

This parable has been problematic throughout our history. For
many years it was interpreted as God's rejection of the Jewish people
and the Christians' superseding of the Jews in the covenant. This
interpretation contributed to our division from the Jewish people,
yielding antisemitism and all the horrors that has caused in our
world. The current interpretation is that the parable condemns the
temple leaders for failure to act justly, their lack of compassion in
laying heavy burdens on others, and their false piety and arrogant
pride.[8]

Of course every parable is a mirror that reveals the audience.
We tend to read parables and interpret them to say that God is on
our side. So if we accept the current interpretation, we see ourselves
coming off as "the good guys." But this doesn't make sense. First,
it doesn't fit the pattern of the gospel as a whole: the merciful shall
obtain mercy, the humble shall be exalted, and Christ came to serve
rather than be served. So a reading of the parable that leads us to
think that we're just fine is probably not valid and certainly isn't
helpful.

Second, it makes the parable irrelevant to us so the living Word
of God is no longer living and active in us. If we read parables and

don't see a call to repentance and reconciliation, that is a pretty clear sign that we have made a false interpretation. Consider this parable of the talents again in a way that makes us uncomfortable.

First, there is the sin of Adam: pride. The tenants want to make themselves the rulers. They want to blot out the owner of the vineyard, disregard their obligations, and claim something for their own that is not rightly theirs. They are repeating the sin of Adam and Eve in the Garden of Eden. How often do we claim as our own achievements those things that are only possible because of those who came before? Our debts are overwhelming, but it is easy to be blind to it and preen in our "own" accomplishments.

Second, the tenants are stealing, claiming the property of others for their own. They were not satisfied with their share of what they produced—they wanted the owner's share too. This parable illustrates the pattern of sin: we start with a lie, that the vineyard belongs to us, and we end up stealing and finally doing violence. So in our daily handling of wealth, if we start with the lie that the money is ours, soon we are cooperating in all kinds of theft and violence: unjust wages, neglect of the poor, and pillaging the creation that gave us our wealth to begin with.

Often we live and work unmindful of our status as tenants and caretakers of creation. We claim gifts freely given by God as our own. We ignore our obligations to the Giver and his intentions that all should share in the bounty of the vineyard, and instead we claim it for ourselves. This parable teaches us the right way to form our hearts. When we live in the truth, that all is gift, and the gifts are to be shared by all, the truth will make us free. We will hold our wealth as a gift and our wealth will no longer own us. These parables provide a pattern for how to live in the world as a Christian. We cannot live the way the advertisers want us to, only thinking of ourselves and our wants. We must make the poor a priority and see to it that we share the goods we have. We cannot excuse ourselves by saying that we pay taxes and the government will take care of the poor.

Mark has a pointed story about the question of taxes. The Pharisees and Herodians asked Jesus if it was lawful to pay taxes to Caesar (Mark 12:13-18). This was a trick question meant to trap Jesus—either he says yes and they can accuse him of cooperating with the Roman oppressors, or he says no and they can accuse him of fomenting revolution. The Lord turns the trap on them, however, by asking whose image is on the coin. "Caesar's," they answer. "Then give to Caesar what is Caesar's," Jesus says, "and to God what is God's." The early theologian Tertullian interpreted this as meaning that one gives Caesar only money, but to God one devotes one's own self, since each of us is the image of God. The church fathers taught that Christians should pay their taxes and pray for their rulers. Clear advice, to be sure—but it requires prayer and thought to translate into deciding which job to take or how to vote.

Applying the gospel to our lives is a process of discernment, testing ideas to see if they are of God or not. We are required to decide what belongs to God and what belongs to Caesar. We have to decide how to live as a disciple of Christ in a world that is very different from the agrarian society of the gospel writers. Fortunately we do not have to do this alone. The Second Vatican Council, in which bishops from around the world met with the pope to discern and teach the faith in the modern world, dealt with these issues and imparted guidance on how to be a disciple today. In the following chapter we look at that council and its teaching on the secular vocation of the laity.

3

Vatican II:
The Council and the Laity

Many Catholics of a certain age remember this council as a revolutionary event: one Sunday we went to Mass in Latin and prayed the rosary like the sisters told us to, and the next Sunday the priest was telling everyone Mass was going to be in English and we all better sing and follow along. The liturgical changes brought about by the Constitution on the Sacred Liturgy (*Sacrosanctum Concilium*), celebrating the Eucharist in the language of the people instead of Latin, made it seem as if the council was changing everything. The old Latin aphorism—*lex orandi, lex credendi* (as we pray, so we believe)—showed its power. We had changed how we prayed so many thought we had changed what we believed.

The council changed Catholic life, we were no longer in our own ghetto. The council's work was not just about the church but about the world. Since the laity are working in the world, the council gave us a new understanding of ourselves and of our place in the church. The council fathers wanted to help Catholics understand their place in the world and their responsibilities to God and their neighbors in the changed circumstances of the twentieth century. To understand the work of the council and its effect on lay life, we begin with a little history and then look at the texts which are most significant for the laypeople called to follow Christ in the world.

Vatican II

On January 25, 1959, on a visit to the Basilica of St. Paul Outside the Walls, Pope John XXIII surprised the cardinals and bishops with an announcement that he was calling an ecumenical council. The Vatican newspaper reported, "In the mind of the Holy Father, the aim of the Council is not simply the spiritual good of the Christian people. It is also an invitation to the separated communities to seek the unity to which so many souls aspire today throughout the whole of the earth."[1]

The council called together some 2,500 bishops from all around the world, as well as observers from other Christian churches. The first session was opened by the pope on October 11, 1962. In his opening address, the pope presented his vision for a council that spoke to the whole world and sought to heal divisions. He asked that the council apply the medicine of compassion and direct its efforts to a fundamental renewal of the universal church, in living dialogue with the present time and its needs.

The bishops met in the Vatican for ten-week sessions each fall from 1962 to 1965. In between these sessions bishops and theologians worked on the documents that were to become the teaching of the church. Pope John's death on June 3, 1963, might have been the end of the council, but the following month Pope Paul VI announced that the council would continue in order to complete its work. He presided at the closing session on December 8, 1965.

The council wrote and the pope promulgated sixteen documents that contain the teaching of the council on a wide range of subjects. Each document has a Latin title that gives the first two words of the text. Dogmatic constitutions are highest in authority, they cover the key concerns of the council: the Constitution on the Sacred Liturgy (*Sacrosanctum Concilium*); the Dogmatic Constitution on Divine Revelation (*Dei Verbum*); and the Dogmatic Constitution on the

Church (*Lumen Gentium*). Next in authority is the Pastoral Constitution on the Church in the Modern World (*Gaudium et Spes*). It is called a *pastoral* rather than a *dogmatic* constitution because it covers issues of the day in addition to doctrine. Nine decrees covered subjects like the bishops (*Christus Dominus*), the ministry of priests (*Presbyterorum Ordinis*), the renewal of religious life (*Perfectae Caritatis*), ecumenism (*Unitatis Redintegratio*), the eastern churches (*Orientalum Ecclesiarum*), and the apostolate of the laity (*Apostolicam Actuositatem*). Finally, there are declarations: on Christian education (*Gravissimum Educationis*); on non-Christian religions (*Nostra Aetate*), and on religious freedom (*Dignitatis Humanae*). Although they are lowest in authority as documents, *Nostra Aetate* and *Dignitatis Humanae* have had an enormous impact on the practical life of the church, especially how laity live out their life in the world.

The church's doctrine proclaims that the pope and the bishops in an ecumenical council are the highest teaching authority in the church. When the council teaches on doctrine, it has the gift (or "charism") of infallibility. Perhaps it is easier to accept this about the Council of Nicaea (325 AD), since we don't know as much about those bishops and their foibles. For the Second Vatican Council, however, there were news reports every day, as groups of theologians and bishops provided press briefings. Of course the narrative morphed into the one we all understand: good guys and bad guys, progressives and conservatives. It wasn't accurate but it made a story that the reporters knew how to write.

The council was a lived experience of the teaching church as the bishops united with the pope. Writing about the council (which he attended as a theologian advising a bishop), Pope Emeritus Benedict XVI remembers: "The Council had caused to be heard the voice of the episcopate—no the voice of the universal Church. For, with and in the bishops, the respective countries, the faithful and their needs and their concerns, were represented."[2] Another of the theologians of the Council, Yves Congar, described it this way:

> I remember reading, a long time ago, in the classical manuals, about the distinction between the episcopate disperse and the episcopate

gathered together. It was a very ordinary subject and I had no suspicion that it dealt with such an important reality. In fact it refers to two different levels of thought—the sociological and the theological. . . . At the theological level, a council is not simply a conference. It consists of men, of course, so that there are tensions and there is manoeuvring [sic]. It consists of pastors. It is a reality of the Church, a celebration and a time when God acts on his people. The Holy Spirit is active at a council and makes this sociological communication into a communion and a unanimity that is concerned with the City of God.[3]

The Second Vatican Council recognized a new identity of the laity; no longer were we defined negatively, as those who are not clerics or religious; we are defined positively as *christifideles*, members of the people of God, called by our baptism and confirmation to holiness. As part of its work, the council expanded the role of the laity in the church and clarified our role in sanctifying the world. In the years immediately following the council, the questions surrounding laypeople working in the church as pastoral associates, liturgists, and directors of religious education—what we now call ecclesial lay ministry—took center stage. New roles in the church for the laity required a new education for those roles. This was a priority to revitalize parish life and so became the major focus of implementing the council's teaching on the laity. The corresponding call of the council that the laity work to make the secular world a place of justice and peace as God desires received less attention, even though it is the way the vast majority of laypeople live their vocation. Fifty years after the council, we have theologically trained laypeople working at all levels of the church. Now it is time to turn again to the council's teaching on the laity in the secular world. To do so we turn first to the teaching about the laity in the Dogmatic Constitution on the Liturgy, *Sacrocanctum Concilium*.

Liturgy and Belief

As we said in the beginning of this book, the perception by the laity that they were the passive sheep was reinforced by the way we worshipped prior to the council. The priest and altar servers proclaimed everything in Latin, while the laity in the pews said their prayers. The Liturgical Movement that began at the end of the nineteenth century had the aim of restoring the liturgy, the public prayer of the church (the Eucharist, especially), to a central place in the piety of the faithful and renewing their active participation in it. This movement bore fruit in the first session of the council. Bishops were debating what to do with the many *schemata* (draft documents) prepared by the Curia, the administrators of the church in the Vatican. They decided to begin with the draft on the sacred liturgy. Pope Emeritus Benedict XVI remembers that this decision was significant because it was the truly central thing in the church, the Eucharist, where the Lord and his church are united. This text implied an entire vision of the church and "thus anticipated (in a degree that cannot be too highly appreciated) the main theme of the entire Council—its teaching on the Church."[4] Among the objectives of this constitution was "a more active participation of the laity; the inclusion of the whole communion of God into a holy fulfillment."[5] The renewed liturgy, in the language we use every day, meant that the laity could be active participants in worship, rather than a passive audience.

The constitution was written with the lay faithful in mind, as can be seen from the opening:

> The sacred Council has set out to impart an ever-increasing vigor to the Christian life of the faithful; to adapt more closely to the needs of our age those institutions which are subject to change; to foster whatever can promote union among all who believe in Christ; to strengthen whatever can help to call all mankind into the Church's fold. Accordingly it sees particularly cogent reasons for undertaking the reform and promotion of the liturgy. For it is the liturgy through which, especially in the divine sacrifice of the Eucharist, "the work of our redemption is accomplished" and it is through the liturgy, especially, that the faithful are enabled to express in their lives and manifest to others the mystery of Christ and the real nature of the true Church. (SC 1–2)

To see how this constitution's vision flowed into the council, we turn first to the Dogmatic Constitution on the Church, *Lumen Gentium*.

From "Not Clergy" to Christ's Faithful People: *Lumen Gentium*

Congar had written a book about the laity in the 1950s that foreshadowed much of what became the council's teaching on the laity. He began his study by first defining laypeople. The definition was itself a negative one: the laity are those who are *not* clerics or in religious vows. The laity have no "part in the power of jurisdiction and especially, of holy order."[6] Holy orders, the sacrament of ordination to the priesthood, was understood to convey to the priest the power to participate in Christ's roles as prophet, priest, and king. The laity were the recipients of his action in these roles: receiving teaching through the priest's prophetic role, receiving graces from the priest's priestly action in the sacraments, and receiving instruction on how the world should be ruled and organized from the priest's kingly role.

The church that Congar described was the church that emerged from the Counter-Reformation. Some Protestant reformers had proposed that there was no need for apostolic succession or a hierarchy of bishops and priests. In order to refute this, the Catholic Church emphasized the hierarchy and the ministerial priesthood in its teaching. This conception of the church as primarily about the clergy is called clericalism, has ill effects, and is still with us, as Congar detailed: "Pastorally clericalism results in this, that lay people, kept in subjection and passivity in the Church, are not formed for their own Christian responsibilities, which it is their business to discharge in the world and in the course of history."[7]

All virtues are reduced to obedience, all sins to sins of the flesh, and the laity excuse themselves from responsibility in the church and in the world. This is a caricature, of course, but too often we still see this in, for example, parents who think that if they send their children to Catholic school, they don't need to do anything else, such as attend Mass on Sunday. Equally we see it when Catholics who have revitalized their faith and want to serve the Lord seek roles in the church rather than taking their excitement about their faith to the workplace, their neighborhood, and other areas of their daily life.

Lumen Gentium's vision of the church adds to the preconciliar teaching, and highlights the importance of baptism and the universal call to holiness. The organization of the constitution itself is instructive. Only after teaching on the mystery of the church (chap. 1) and the people of God (chap. 2) does the document discuss the hierarchy (chap. 3) and the laity (chap. 4). Then it turns to the universal call to holiness in the church (chap. 5) before discussing the religious (chap. 6). It concludes with the union of the pilgrim church on earth with the church in heaven (chap. 7) and finally the Blessed Virgin Mary, mother of God, in the mystery of Christ and the church (chap. 8).

Lumen Gentium identifies the church as "the community of faith, hope and charity, as a visible organization through which he [Christ] communicates truth and grace to all men. . . . This Church, constituted and organized as a society in the present world subsists in the Catholic Church. . . . Nevertheless, many elements of sanctification are found outside its visible confines" (LG 8). This sentence tears down the wall between fortress Catholicism and the other Christian churches and provides a foundation for the documents on ecumenism, relations with non-Christian religions, and religious freedom.

Chapter 2 is titled "The People of God" and begins: "At all times and in every race, anyone who fears God and does what is right has been acceptable to him (cf. Acts 10:35)" (LG 9). Instead of emphasizing the separation of Catholics from others, it recognizes God's love of all his creatures. It continues: "Christ instituted this new covenant, . . . he called a race made up of Jews and Gentiles which would be one, not according to the flesh, but in the Spirit, and this race would be the new People of God" (LG 9). Everyone in the people of God has a mission, as *Lumen Gentium* states: "All the disciples of Christ, persevering in prayer and praising God (cf. Acts 2:42-47), should present themselves as a sacrifice, living, holy and pleasing to God (cf. Rom 12:1). They should everywhere on earth bear witness to Christ and give an answer to everyone who asks a reason for the hope of an eternal life which is theirs (cf. 1 Peter 3:15)" (LG 10). The one mission of all Christians comes from our baptism. This sacrament makes the baptized Christ's faithful people, then we live out this mission within the church in one of many roles: bishop, priest, religious, layperson.

Lumen Gentium includes the laity as sharers in the priestly, prophetic, and kingly functions of Christ, though the way we live this out is different from the way priests do. Our priestly role is to offer God worship and praise through our participation in the sacraments, and our prayer and sacrifices in life (LG 11). Our prophetic role is to be a sign of hope in the world and in the church. We have the anointing of the Holy Spirit, not only in the sacraments but also in special graces that the Holy Spirit distributes "among the faithful of every rank. By these gifts he makes them fit and ready to undertake various tasks and offices for the renewal and building up of the Church" (LG 12). Within the church the laity "are empowered—indeed sometimes obliged—to manifest their opinions on those things which pertain to the good of the Church" (LG 37). Finally, our kingly role is to work to make the world a place of justice. The constitution asks pastors to "recognize and promote the dignity and responsibility of the laity in the Church" while recognizing their freedom to undertake work on their own initiative (LG 37). Clearly, we are no longer the passive recipients of the church's ministry but active members of the communion with our own specific mission.

Most laity will live out their mission in the world, and the document emphasizes the secular nature of our call: "What specifically characterizes the laity is their secular nature. . . . The laity, by their very vocation, seek the kingdom of God by engaging in temporal affairs and by ordering them according to the plan of God. . . . Therefore, since they are tightly bound up in all types of temporal affairs it is their special task to order and to throw light upon these affairs in such a way that they may come into being and then continually increase according to Christ to the praise of the Creator and the Redeemer (LG 31)."

The bishops didn't want to draw a line between the church and the world, assigning the church to the ordained and the world to the laity; however, they recognized that, because laypeople live and work in the world, we have special knowledge and skills that help us in our life there. Since we have the graces of the sacraments and knowledge of the world, it is our job to use our talents and creativity to bring the world closer to God's plan for it, rather than just turn away from it as a place of temptation.

As we have seen, the council opened the way for the laity to undertake roles in the church, but that will not be most laypeoples' primary call. Most of us are to bring Christ to the world. We have to do this while respecting the autonomy of others and by respecting the logic of the temporal world: "For it must be admitted that the temporal sphere is governed by its own principles, since it is rightly concerned with the interests of this world" (LG 36). We can't win an argument in the workplace by saying, "God wants it this way." We have to respect other people and find common ground to convince them to work for justice.

The council calls all of us to holiness; it is no longer just for the A-team, the priests and religious: "It is therefore quite clear that all Christians in any state or walk of life are called to the fullness of Christian life and to the perfection of love, and by this holiness a more human manner of life is fostered also in earthly society" (LG 40). All of us are called to be saints, real saints in the world. We may think this is strange because we only know stories about saints who seemed to be more superhero than spiritual guide. However, this is the reason the church exists: to produce sons and daughters who offer praise and worship to God. This call to holiness means that our vocation touches all parts of our lives, and that our lives need to have a unity in our identity as a Christian.

Since our vocation is in the world, working to make it just and developing the potential of each person and the goods of creation, we are immersed in the world. We can't forget that God called us to do this, but even so earth is not our final home. This is the challenge for lay Christians: to live in the world, care for the world, and yet remember that it will pass away when God's kingdom comes in its fullness at the end of time. The relationship between the world, the earthly or temporal sphere, and the church was one of the central concerns of the council. The Pastoral Constitution on the Church in the Modern World, *Gaudium et Spes*, expands on the teaching of *Lumen Gentium* and brings it to the situation of the world.

Gaudium et Spes

The very existence of this document is evidence of how different this council was to the ones that preceded it. The struggles to create the document show us how hard it is to do something in a new way. A description of some of these struggles illustrates the importance of the constitution and of our role as laity in the world.

Before Vatican II, ecumenical councils dealt with doctrine such as the full divinity and humanity of Christ in one person, or with disciplinary matters such as clerical celibacy. Councils defined dogma and condemned heresy. Doctrine was truth and was unchanging. Doctrine and heresy were the special expertise of the church, or at least of her bureaucrats in the Curia. The commissions who prepared documents for the Second Vatican Council to debate when it convened were made up primarily of these bureaucrats. They thought in the traditional pattern, that the council was about doctrine, rather than earthly realities.

In the first session, the council fathers had to debate the 70 drafts (*schemata*) prepared by these commissions. The bishops were not happy with them. They wanted them to be fewer in number and written in the way that Pope John had asked the council to act: ecumenically—that is, in fraternal charity with other Christians—and pastorally, offering the medicine of mercy rather than the harsh condemnations of theological errors. On December 4, 1962, Cardinal Suenens made a speech proposing to group the *schemata* around two poles: inside, the church; and outside, the world.[8] The bishops realized that Pope John from the very beginning had aimed at openness to the world—for example, in his Pentecost sermon on June 5, 1960, where he said, "Each believer . . . as far as he is Catholic, is a citizen of the whole world, just as Christ is the adored redeemer of the whole world."[9] The first session ended with the original *schemata* sent back for redrafting by the preparatory commissions in line with Pope John's understanding of the council. New commissions were formed to revise, rewrite, and rethink the documents for the council.

No laity had participated in the preparatory commissions, since they were organized by curial officials who thought of ecumenical councils as consisting of bishops advised by theologians. This meant that the church couldn't really enter into dialogue with the world and prepare a meaningful document about the world. The new commission charged with developing Schema XIII (which eventually became

Gaudium et Spes) asked for lay involvement. In March 1964 the first layman addressed the commission. From November 16, 1964, to January 31, 1965, laywomen and nuns also took part in the discussions of the commission as auditors. They weren't allowed to speak in the official deliberations of the council, however.[10] The archbishop of Kraków, Msgr. Karol Wojtyla (later Pope John Paul II), helped draft the document and introduced one of its central ideas—that "the presence of the Church does not consist only in the will of God but also in the will of those who freely belong to it."[11] This became a key idea, marking the importance of the members of the church, meaning priests, religious, *and* laity.

After many heated debates and revisions, including a substantive contribution by the auditors from the World Council of Churches, the Pastoral Constitution of the Church in the Modern World (*Gaudium et Spes*) was accepted by the council. Again, it is called a *pastoral* rather than a *doctrinal* constitution because it deals with the changing realities of the culture; it is the church's response to contemporary concerns. It is a very general document, addressing all of humanity rather than a select portion (such as the church or clergy). Unlike doctrinal constitutions, the very nature of this pastoral document deals with changing realities. Since it is a constitution of an ecumenical council, it is supposed to be valid teaching for the whole church for all time. That is not possible when dealing with changing realties in human culture. The document solved this problem to some degree by having two parts: "The Church and Man's Vocation," which discusses the dignity of the human person, human activity in the world, and the role of the church in the modern world (unchanging doctrines); and "Some Urgent Problems" with its chapters on marriage and the family, development of culture, economic and social life, political community, and international relations and the fostering of peace (the changing realities of life). By separating the two, the static from the variable, the bishops allowed for the doctrinal teaching to be applied to new circumstances that arose as cultures change.

Gaudium et Spes opens: "The joy and hope, the grief and anguish of the men of our time, especially of those who are poor or afflicted

in any way are the joy and hope, the grief and anguish of the followers of Christ as well" (GS 1). This immediately sets the tone for the
document: in addressing problems in the world, it reaches out to all
people, not just Catholics. And it makes clear that both the church
and the temporal world have their rightful place in God's creation.
It identifies the continuing problem in the world as sin: "Therefore
man is split within himself. As a result, all of human life, whether
individual or collective, shows itself to be a dramatic struggle between good and evil, between light and darkness" (GS 13). This is the
context for our earthly life, and the challenge for every generation.

The constitution emphasized the independence of the secular
sphere, by rooting it in creation when God gave all things "their own
stability, truth, goodness, proper laws and order" (GS 36). There is
no split between faith and reason, for "whoever labors to penetrate
the secrets of reality with a humble and steady mind, even though
he is unaware of the fact, is nevertheless being led by the hand of
God, who holds all things in existence and gives them their identity"
(GS 36). The work in the temporal order is valued, but it is different
from the work of the church: "Christ did not bequeath to the Church
a mission in the political, economic or social order: the purpose he
assigned to it was a religious one" (GS 42).

The world needs Christians who know their faith and live it in
their families, their workplaces, in politics and in communal life.
The council calls us to responsible living, according to our state in
life and our call. We cannot neglect earthly duties, nor can we "im-
merse ourselves in earthly activities as if these latter were utterly
foreign to religion" (GS 43). The bishops explicitly deplored the split
between faith and life:

> One of the gravest errors of our time is the dichotomy between the
> faith which many profess and the practice of their daily lives. . . .
> The Christian who shirks his temporal duties, shirks his duties
> toward his neighbor, neglects God himself and endangers his eternal
> salvation. Let Christians follow the example of Christ who worked
> as a craftsman; let them be proud of the opportunity to carry out
> their earthly activity in such a way as to integrate human, domes-
> tic, professional, scientific and technical enterprises with religious

values, under whose supreme direction all things are ordered to the glory of God. (GS 43)

Our work in the world, creating and sustaining a family, making things, and participating in society, helps build up creation, and at the same time it fulfills our call to devote ourselves to the service of others. As the document states: "We believe by faith that through the homage of work offered to God man is associated with the redemptive work of Jesus Christ whose labor with his hands at Nazareth greatly ennobled the dignity of work. This is the source of everyman's duty to work loyally as well as his right to work" (GS 67).

Gaudium et Spes concludes by noting that the document is meant for all, whether they believe in God or not. The purpose was to make "the world conform better to the surpassing dignity of man, to strive for a more deeply rooted sense of universal brotherhood, and to meet the pressing appeals of our time with a generous and common effort of love" (GS 91). The fathers note that their program is general because they are dealing with matters that are changing.

Gaudium et Spes laid out the general theological framework and the principles of the social teaching of the church. This complements well the teaching of *Lumen Gentium*—that all the baptized share in the mission of the church in their own ways. The question of exactly how the laity live out their vocation in the family, in the economic, political, and social spheres, and in the church was the work of the commission on the laity, which produced the Decree on the Apostolate of Lay People (*Apostolicam Actuositatem*), to which we now turn.

Apostolicam Actuositatem

The Decree on the Apostolate of Lay People begins by defining our call, "The Church was founded to spread the kingdom of Christ over all the earth for the glory of God the Father, to make all men partakers in redemption and salvation, and through them to establish the right relationship of the entire world to Christ. . . . In fact the Christian vocation is, of its nature, a vocation to the apostolate as well" (AA 2).

This is the heart of *Apostolicam Actuositatem*. It builds on the theology of church from *Lumen Gentium* and then explains (1) how to live out the universal call to holiness as a layperson, (2) the spiritual formation we need, and (3) the way that lay organizations relate to the church. It is important that it uses the word *apostolate* for lay activity—that means we are working as the apostles did to bring Christ's saving help to everyone in our life. Using this word for lay activity, even when it was not part of official church organizations but part of our ordinary daily life, was a recognition of the new vision of church—and laity within the church—as defined in *Lumen Gentium*.

Apostolicam Actuositatem is careful not to make separations between clergy and laity, church and world, as though laity are only concerned with the world and the clergy with the church. That being said, the document recognizes that "laymen ought to take on themselves as their distinctive task this renewal of the temporal order . . . everywhere and always they have to seek the justice of the kingdom of God" (AA 7). Some laity may be called to work with or for the church: "Finally the hierarchy entrusts the laity with certain charges more closely connected with the duties of pastors: in the teaching of Christian doctrine, for example, in certain liturgical actions, in the care of souls" (AA 24). In discerning our own individual call, even if most of the time we are working in the world, we must be open to service in the church, in the parish or diocese.

To understand the document we have to look at its context, Catholic Action and other lay organizations. Catholic Action was the name for an organization that, particularly during the nineteenth century, worked in the temporal sphere (especially politics) under the direction of the hierarchy. Its mission was to bring Christianity to the secular realm under the direction of the bishop. Catholic Action became very important in response to anti-Catholic and anti-clerical governments in Europe. As Catholic Action grew in importance, however, there was a perceived conflict between it and other lay organizations, such as spiritual associations, third orders, guilds, the Society of the Holy Name, and so on. The Commission on the Laity was to settle these disputes and define how lay associations related to the church. In the discussions on this document, "at stake was the issue of a mandate required of those acting officially in the name of the Church and the freedom and right of lay people to 'form organizations, manage them and join them, provided they maintain the proper relationship with ecclesiastical authority.'"[12]

This question—whether the laity need to work in the secular sphere under the authority of the bishop or whether they have a rightful autonomy in their apostolate in the world—was key in the deliberations that produced this document. In the course of its deliberation the commission recognized that there were a variety of ways that laypeople took their rightful place in advancing the mission of the church, and that we as laity do have a rightful autonomy—especially when dealing with secular affairs in which the laity have specialist knowledge. It also acknowledged that the laity have an apostolate as individuals and not just as members of a lay group or association.

The document is perhaps most useful to us in the details it provides of the various fields of the apostolate (chap. 3), the different forms of the apostolate (chap. 4), and the formation for apostolate (chap. 6). The questions of order and relations of lay organizations with the church have been taken up into the new Code of Canon Law and, generally speaking, do not concern us unless we are founding a new lay society and desire official church recognition.

The council fathers took a wide view of the fields of the apostolate, and it is worth looking in detail at what was said. We have responsibilities to the church community: "[the laity] ardently cooperate in the spread of the Word of God, particularly by catechetical instruction; by their expert assistance they increase the efficacy of the care of souls as well as of the administration of the goods of the Church" (AA 10). We are not to think only of our parish but remember that we are part of a diocese, and of the people of God spread throughout the world.

The family has the mission of "being the primary vital cell of society" (AA 11). Young people should be witnesses to other young people, and "children, too, have an apostolate of their own. In their own measure they are the true living witnesses of Christ among their companions" (AA 12). This is the principle of the apostolate of like toward like. This is especially appropriate in trying "to infuse the

Christian spirit into the mentality and behavior, laws and structures of the community in which one lives. . . . It is amid the surroundings of their work that they are best qualified to be of help to their brothers, in the surroundings of their profession, of their study, residence, leisure, or local group" (AA 13). We are to be good citizens of our country and of the world, remembering our bonds of solidarity with all people, by working for the common good.

There is no sphere of life exempt from our call to witness to Christ by our words and actions. We are called to this both as individuals and as members of a group, be it a parish community, our place of residence, secular groups like the PTA or Rotary Club, or church groups, such as the Christian Family Movement or Catholic Lawyers Guild.

Finally, the document reminds us that to be effective we need training; in fact, the fathers recommend something like a total quality improvement process. We are never finished learning about God and his kingdom, and so improving our work as witnesses to Christ. We need "spiritual formation, solid grounding in doctrine" in order to "*see* all things in the light of faith, to *judge* and *act* always in its light, and to improve and perfect oneself by working with others and in this manner to enter actively into the service of the Church" (AA 29, emphasis added). This see–judge–act structure came from the Young Christian Worker movement, which was founded by Joseph Cardinal Cardijn after World War II and provided a major influence on this document. It gives us a way to approach our lives and weave together the disparate strands of our apostolate into a unity.

We live and work in a multi-faith world; most of the Catholic ghettos have disappeared. The council recognized this reality and thought through its own teaching on the dignity of each human person. The result was the Declaration on Religious Liberty, *Dignitatis Humanae*.

Dignitatis Humanae

Our mission is lived in a society with people of many faiths and some with no faith at all. The task of witnessing to Christ in a pluralist society is greatly helped by the document on religious liberty. It is a declaration, which has the lowest authority of the conciliar documents, but it has had a great impact on the experience of the church. To understand it we must go back to fortress Catholicism, in which the church was right, everyone else was wrong, and the motto was *extra ecclesiam nulla salus* (outside the church there is no salvation). The council had to find a way to protect the fact that the church possesses the revelation of Christ but also recognizes the freedom of individual conscience. The push for such a declaration came not only from the Western (liberal) churches but also from the church in Communist countries.

The document manages to do this by opening with the statement that the "one true religion continues to exist in the Catholic and Apostolic Church," and that humanity is bound to seek the truth. But truth cannot be imposed by force, it must win the mind. Therefore we have a right to religious freedom:

> This Vatican Council declares that the human person has a right to religious freedom. Freedom of this kind means that all men are to be immune from coercion on the part of individuals, social groups and every human power so that, within due limits, nobody is forced to act against his convictions nor is anyone to be restrained from acting in accordance with his convictions in religious matters in private or in public, alone or in associations with others. The Council further declares that the right to religious freedom is based on the very dignity of the human person as known through the revealed word of God and by reason itself. This right of the human person to religious freedom must be given such recognition in the constitutional order of society as will make it a civil right. (DH 2)

This document, along with the Decree on Ecumenism (*Unitatis Redintegratio*) and the Declaration on the Relation of the Church to Non-Christian Religions (*Nostrae Aetate*), gives us the task of respecting others' conscience, working with them for the common good, and witnessing to them of the hope we have in us through Christ. This is a difficult balancing act between tolerance for others and the command of Christ to make all people disciples.

We can have a true dialogue with other believers and with non-believers only when we are knowledgeable about our own beliefs and open to hearing about the other's beliefs. It is a tension that both sides of the dialogue believe their religion is true; and we do not serve God or each other if we try to pretend the differences do not exist or that they are not important.

As difficult as that is, though, our witness is stronger when we have a deep respect for the consciences of others and realize that we must be a witness with our lives and not just with our words. We won't go far wrong when we act in ways that increase love and respect for all people.

Conclusion

The Second Vatican Council gave us the tools we need to live out our secular vocation in a multicultural, multi-faith world. We are called to be active participants—not passive recipients—in the liturgy of the church (*Sacrosanctum Concilium*). Our place is both in the church and in the world as disciples of Christ, joined to him through our baptism (*Lumen Gentium*). We are to bring all parts of our life into a unity of love and service to God and our neighbor and not live a divided life with faith separate from all other aspects of our life (*Gaudium et Spes*). We are to recognize our ability to witness to others in our daily life, in the common things of life, our family, our workplaces, our community, and the parish and diocese. How we live is as important as what we say (*Apostolicam Actuositatem*). And, finally, we respect all people and their right to religious freedom, while witnessing to our own belief in Christ (*Dignitatis Humanae*).

From these documents we should gain a new appreciation of our role in the church and our call to be witnesses to Christ. Fifty years after the council, our witness is needed by the world more than ever. Today people convert to Christianity only after a long process: trusting a Christian, becoming curious, opening up to change, seeking after God, and entering the kingdom.[13] As laypeople we are very likely to be the Christians that inspire others to become seekers. This gives a new urgency to the council's idea of each of us giving a witness of life. To be the kind of Christian that people trust, we must be authentically Christian and authentically ourselves.

Each of us is a unique creation of God with gifts, talents, and needs, born into a particular time and place. Each of us has work to do. The prayer attributed to St. Teresa of Avila says it best: "Christ has no body now but yours. No hands, no feet on earth but yours." We need to use our mind to discover how to integrate our life and use our particular talents in our discipleship. The following chapter has some exercises to help us discover ways that we can be an effective disciple and locate the places where our talents can meet the world's needs.

chapter 4

Discovering My Call

The teaching of Vatican II shows us that we are called to follow Christ in all areas of our life. Each of us has a special contribution to make. We are to work with the talents that God gave us, not ignore them. In this chapter you will investigate what special gifts and talents you are to use in your vocation. We begin with the theology of the person as the image of God, gifted with spiritual gifts and called to be a steward of creation. Then we turn to some exercises to discover our particular gifts. Finally, there are tools for evaluating our goals in light of what the church teaches about how to create a society of justice and peace, known as Catholic Social Teaching.

The Image of God

We are made in the image of God and bear this image in our ability to love others, in our self-consciousness, our memory, and in our ability to create. We are not clones; we are unique individuals. Those particular facts about each of us—including our family and the time and place we were born—mean that each of us has a unique call to make God known. We have different abilities, personalities, and situations. God created a diverse world, made us stewards of creation, and now desires everyone to help in their own way in their time and place.

As I look at the natural world, I am convinced that God really likes variety. It is the same with people. Each one of us is unique, unrepeatable, and has something to contribute to building up the kingdom of God as we live in the world. As you work through the exercises that follow, I hope you discover the special gifts and talents you have, whether it is being patient, organized, caring for others, or producing beautiful music, impressive art, or great food. We are multitalented, multifaceted people who have much to give our world. As Christians we are called to make right the things that are wrong in that world—protect the innocent, heal the sick, shelter the homeless, bury the dead, protect the environment, get people out of poverty, and change the systems that oppress so many. None of us can do everything, but everyone can do something, and together we can accomplish great things.

By completing the following exercises you will discover more about your personality and the talents that God gave you. This raw material is enriched and changed by the grace we receive in the sacraments. In our baptism we become members of the church. We are purified from sin and we receive sanctifying grace from the Holy Trinity. This gives us the power to live and act under the prompting of the Holy Spirit through the gifts of the Holy Spirit. This grace enables us to grow in goodness, developing these gifts and the virtues. Confirmation strengthens these gifts in us. The church's tradition has identified the seven gifts of the Spirit as knowledge, wisdom, understanding, counsel, reverence (piety), fortitude (courage), and wonder and awe in God's presence (fear of the Lord).

When I was teaching this in religious education classes, students were surprised about how many of the gifts related to thinking: knowledge, wisdom, understanding, and counsel. Knowledge is the gift of knowing about God; wisdom means we give the right value to the things of faith; understanding means we don't just know the words but comprehend how God's grace works in our lives and in the life of the church; and counsel means we have developed the virtue of prudence so that we know how to act in difficult situations. We know, understand, and treasure the great gift we have received in becoming children of God. Reverence, wonder, and awe in God's presence mean that we recognize the goodness and greatness of God and our smallness, yet trust in his love. Finally, fortitude is the kind of courage that holds on to these things even when we are plagued by doubts, people are laughing at us, or killing us for the faith, as the martyrs experienced.

God gives us the gifts, but that doesn't mean he takes away our freedom. He has given us a desire to share in his life, a God-shaped hole in the center of our life, and he is prepared to fill it with as much love as we can hold. One of the early church fathers, St. Irenaeus, described it as divinization: the Word of God "did . . . become what we are, that He might bring us to be even what He is Himself."[1] These gifts were given to us so that we may produce the fruits of the Spirit: love, joy, peace, patience, kindness, goodness, generosity, gentleness, faithfulness, modesty, self-control, and chastity (CCC 1832). The first in the list is love, since God is love. This means the love that wants the best for the other person, not the feeling that quickly becomes self-indulgent and excuses all kinds of bad behavior. The ultimate model of this love is the cross, because Jesus loved us so much he himself bore all the consequences of our sins. It is that self-sacrificing love that each of us is called to bring to reality in our lives.

Socrates tells us that wisdom begins when we know ourselves. It is so easy under the pressure of living and paying the bills to skip the big picture and concentrate on getting through the week instead. Then we find ourselves unhappy and unfulfilled. The exercises in this chapter provide a chance to step back, reflect on who you are, identify your gifts, and locate where you are in life. God gave you these raw materials and wants you to be joyful in your work and life as you build God's kingdom. Of course there will be times of trial and sorrow, but we are not supposed to make life more difficult for ourselves than it already is.

Personality

Our basic material is our personality or temperament. We tolerate change, or we hate it; we like to be with people talking, or we like to think quietly by ourselves; we are focused on the results, or we are more concerned about the process of getting something done. The ancient Greeks divided people into temperaments based on four bodily fluids. The science was bad, but the classification into four types is instantly recognizable: the melancholic, introspective and focused on details; the choleric, ambitious and driven; the phlegmatic, consistent and content; and the sanguine, sociable and pleasure seeking. A recent work on communication styles maps four types that are very similar: analytics (melancholic), drivers (choleric), amiables (phlegmatic), and expressives (sanguine).[2]

When I presented the communication styles activity to a large group of people I asked them to sit with others who were the same type and, as a group, identify their strengths and weaknesses as team members at work. As I observed the room, I found the analytics were all seated in a tight circle with legs crossed, each with a notebook, writing down whatever anyone in the group said. The drivers were loud, finished the assigned task within half of the allotted time, and complained about waiting for the other groups to finish. The amiables had made a large, inclusive circle of their chairs and were listening to each other with great attention and head nodding. They were still introducing themselves by the time the rest of the groups had finished the task. The expressives were laughing and talking, making an attempt at doing the assigned task, but equally involved in enjoying being social. In management training this exercise is important because it shows us that all four types of people are equally good and equally necessary for any good team. In life outside of work it is helpful to understand why we seem to instantly bond with some people and find it hard to deal with others.

Analytics/melancholic	Drivers/choleric
detail oriented/introspective	task oriented/ambitious and driven
Amiables/phlegmatic	Expressives/sanguine
process oriented/consistent and contented	communication oriented/sociable and pleasure seeking

Maybe you recognize yourself in one of the types. Of course most people are a mixture, but each of us has a dominant style. The diagram gives you a rough guide to your primary temperament. For me, as an expressive, writing and public speaking are enjoyable, even though they require a lot of work. My life and work satisfaction increased when I realized just how important this is to me, and in my fifties I got my doctorate and a teaching position at a university. I look forward to going to work that fits who I am, and to me that is a daily blessing.

Exercise 1: Personality type
Think about how you like to work and communicate with others. Can you position yourself in one of the quadrants? Most likely you are a mixture, but try to identify your dominant style.

Talents

As I went through the process of discerning whether to go to graduate school—especially considering the time and financial commitment as a very mature student—I used a fairly simple process. I looked back at my life and analyzed what was satisfying for me and what was difficult. It was easier because I had enjoyed what is politely called a "portfolio career"—that is, fewer full-time jobs and more consulting, freelance, and part-time positions that were varied. Even if you have been in one job for many years, you have had multiple experiences both at work and in your personal relationships that can help you identify your talents. The first step is to examine the jobs or volunteer positions you have held.

Exercise 2: Job analysis
Go through your resume and give each position its own sheet of paper, listing the good and bad things about that position. Be specific. For example, I was an assistant magazine editor. On balance I enjoyed the work of editing and learned a tremendous amount from that job, but when it ended I deliberately looked for work that would involve more work with other people and less work that had to be

done by myself. Be sure to include a sheet for your work as student, volunteer, mother, father, or spouse. Here are two examples:

Assistant Editor	
fulfilling /easy to do	*tedious/hard to do*
working with authors	detail work of copyediting
tracking the work flow	proofreading
editing a piece while maintaining the author's voice	most work done alone
learning the process of page layout and new software	too much detail work in copyediting
meeting new people	small office, not enough human interaction
learning new things	

Den Mother	
fulfilling /easy to do	*tedious/hard to do*
designing the activities for the year to ensure the boys achieved Wolf Cub	detail work of record keeping
prepping the meetings	fundraising
working with the cubs	keeping cubs on task
meeting new people in the neighborhood	Pinewood Derby
developing new friendships	
public speaking	

Create your own grids for positions you have held that you believe yield important information about yourself. When you have finished, look over them and see if any consistent themes appear (on either side of the page). Identify any common threads that make tasks either fulfilling or tedious for you. Looking at the two sample charts above, detail work appears on the tedious side in both. This doesn't mean that I get to choose jobs that are free of detail work (if such jobs even existed), but it means that I should be careful not to take on a position that is primarily about getting the details right.

Exercise 3: Peak experiences

Identify two or three of the best things you have done in your life. They do not have to be employment related; they may be events in one's personal life or achievements in one's hobbies that yield some of our best experiences. Jot down what made these events or accomplishments so satisfying.

Exercise 4: Learning from failure

Identify two or three major failures in your life. What went wrong? What can you learn from this in terms of your talents? Were you a square peg in a round hole? When I served as the president of the Home School Association I found that I could do the job, but I did not pay enough attention to building consensus and involving more people in the organization. I had responsibility but not control. I disliked being constantly on call and the recipient of everyone's complaints. This taught me that I am much happier when I am a follower rather than the leader, and I prefer having definite tasks that are under my control, like producing a newsletter.

Exercise 5: Strengths and weaknesses

Choose five words that define your strengths and five that you consider your weaknesses. Think about what others say about you. Now ask your spouse, best friend, or mentor to do the same. Compare the lists.

	Strength words	Weakness words
1.		
2.		
3.		
4.		
5.		

Exercise 6: Putting it together

Look over the five exercises you have completed. How do the tasks you find fulfilling relate to your peak experiences? When you look at your failures, compare them to the tedious tasks you iden tified. Do the word lists you and your partner made confirm the talents and strengths that you see? Make your identification of your talents as general as you can, rather than tying them to concrete jobs or experiences you have had. These are the important building blocks of your vocation. So, for example, one of my peak experiences was presenting research on the state of children in Connecticut to a large (100+) audience, one of my strength words is "passionate," and one of the things I enjoyed in Cub Scouts was public speaking. So I listed public speaking/presenting as one of my talents. Make a list of your own talents.

Exercise 7: Talents and vocation

The talents you have are useful not just in work life, but in all areas of your vocation. To see how that works, look at the following matrix. In the first column of the matrix, write the talents you have identified as your strengths. Under each of the four areas of living your vocation, identify which talents you are using, and which talents are not being used. If, for example, you are in an administrative job but your talent is communicating with people, under talents your gift would be communication, and under work you might note that it was being used, but not to its full capacity. But in your relationships perhaps it appears as a great strength. Note where you think your talents might enrich various areas of your life.

Areas of living your vocation					
Spiritual community					
Civic community					
Relationships					
Work					
Talents					

Values

The talents and temperament we have are, to some extent, given to us. As we grow up in a family and community we develop our values. Having grown up in a very small town, I really value privacy now! Looking at values gives us a better sense of ourselves. The Rokeach Values Survey was developed by Milton Rokeach, a social psychologist who researched racial prejudice and, more generally, human values. The survey appeared in his book *The Nature of Human Values*, a work that has been very influential in the psychological study of values. More recently, his work has been used by market researchers to understand consumers better. It is also a useful tool toward determining one's vocation, as God's call includes the values we hold (and the order in which we hold them).

Exercise 8: The Rokeach Values Survey

There are two lists of values—terminal values and instrumental values   for you to rate. Read through each list, and think about each value in terms of its importance to you as a guiding principle in your life. Is it of greater importance to you, lesser importance, or somewhere in-between?

Rate each of the values in terms of their importance to you by entering the appropriate number (1 = of lesser importance, 7 = of greater importance) in the column marked **No**. As you work, consider each value in relation to all the other values listed on each chart. Work slowly and think carefully about the importance you assign to all the values listed. All of the values are good choices, but we learn about ourselves from the relative weights we assign to them.

Transfer the number you have given each value to the appropriate shaded box. For example, your score for "a sense of accomplishment" goes under the Personal Scores column, your score for "a world at peace" goes under the Social Scores column. In the second set, the Instrumental Values, you follow the same procedure. Total your scores in each of the columns. (Calculators are allowed!)

Terminal Values	Of lesser importance			Of greater importance			No.	Personal Scores	Social Scores
A comfortable life	1	2	3	4	5	6	7			
An exciting life	1	2	3	4	5	6	7			
A sense of accomplishment	1	2	3	4	5	6	7			
A world at peace	1	2	3	4	5	6	7			
A world of beauty	1	2	3	4	5	6	7			
Equality	1	2	3	4	5	6	7			
Family security	1	2	3	4	5	6	7			
Freedom	1	2	3	4	5	6	7			
Happiness	1	2	3	4	5	6	7			
Inner harmony	1	2	3	4	5	6	7			
Mature love	1	2	3	4	5	6	7			
National security	1	2	3	4	5	6	7			
Pleasure	1	2	3	4	5	6	7			
Salvation	1	2	3	4	5	6	7			
Self-respect	1	2	3	4	5	6	7			
Social recognition	1	2	3	4	5	6	7			
True friendship	1	2	3	4	5	6	7			
Wisdom	1	2	3	4	5	6	7			
							Total		

Instrumental Values	Of lesser importance				Of greater importance			No.	Competence Scores	Moral Scores
Ambitious	1	2	3	4	5	6	7			
Broadminded	1	2	3	4	5	6	7			
Capable	1	2	3	4	5	6	7			
Cheerful	1	2	3	4	5	6	7			
Clean	1	2	3	4	5	6	7			
Courageous	1	2	3	4	5	6	7			
Forgiving	1	2	3	4	5	6	7			
Helpful	1	2	3	4	5	6	7			
Honest	1	2	3	4	5	6	7			
Imaginative	1	2	3	4	5	6	7			
Independent	1	2	3	4	5	6	7			
Intellectual	1	2	3	4	5	6	7			
Logical	1	2	3	4	5	6	7			
Loving	1	2	3	4	5	6	7			
Obedient	1	2	3	4	5	6	7			
Polite	1	2	3	4	5	6	7			
Responsible	1	2	3	4	5	6	7			
Self-controlled	1	2	3	4	5	6	7			
							Total			

Once you have ranked your values, you can determine your values scores. First, add the scores in the shaded boxes of each table, and then perform the calculations as shown in the following tables.

Terminal Values	
Divide the total in the Personal column by 53. This is your Personal Score.	
Divide the total in the Social column by 18. This is your Social Score.	-
Subtract the Social Score from the Personal Score for your Terminal Values score. A positive number indicates a "personal" orientation; a negative number indicates a "social" orientation.	

Instrumental Values	
Divide the total in the Competence column by 36. This is your Competence Score.	
Divide the total in the Moral column by 30. This is your Moral Score.	-
Subtract the Moral Score from the Competence Score for your Instrumental Values score. A positive number indicates a "competence" orientation; a negative number indicates a "moral" orientation.	

For example, Mary had a Personal total of 301, which was a score of 5.7; and a Social total of 37, which produced a score of 2.1. Therefore, her Terminal values score was 3.6. Her competence total was 170 for a score of 4.7, and her moral total was 202 for a score of 6.7. So her Instrumental values score was -2.

The next step is plotting your scores on a grid.

		Terminal Values															
		Personal Values								Social Values							
Instrumental Values	Competence Values								+7								
									+6								
									+5								
									+4								
									+3								
									+2								
									+1								
		+7	+6	+5	+4	+3	+2	+1	0	-1	-2	-3	-4	-5	-6	-7
	Moral Values								-1								
									-2								
									-3								
									-4								
									-5								
									-6								
									-7								

When you plot Mary's numbers, 3,6 and -2,0, the intersection is in the Personal and Moral quadrant.

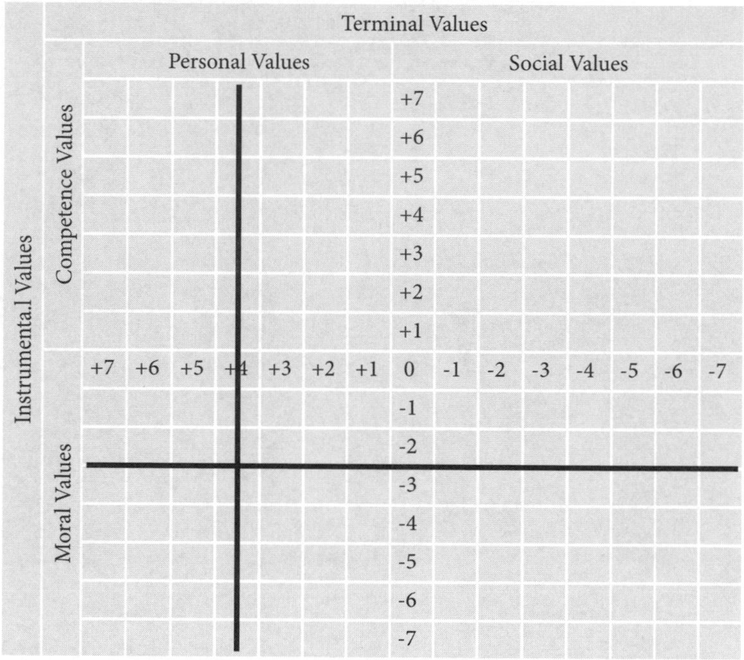

		Terminal Values												
		Personal Values						Social Values							
							+7								
							+6								
							+5								
							+4								
							+3								
							+2								
							+1								
+7	+6	+5	+4	+3	+2	+1	0	-1	-2	-3	-4	-5	-6	-7
							-1								
							-2								
							-3								
							-4								
							-5								
							-6								
							-7								

Left axis labels: Instrumental Values; Competence Values (upper); Moral Values (lower)

This exercise shows you what type of values are most important to you. All of the values are good choices; the interesting thing is what weight we give them. The terminal values show us what we care about. Mary found that although she valued the choices that make up the social score—a world of beauty, peace, and equality—she didn't rate them as a 6 or 7 because they seemed beyond her control. This doesn't mean she didn't care about these things, but she tended to be a follower rather than the leader of a cause. She would recycle and save energy, but she would give more of her time to developing friendships.

The instrumental values show us what kind of person we *want* to be, and since all are good choices it is important to look at why you gave each value the number you did. This is a more detailed way of finding out what we really want—and sometimes we are carrying a load of "supposed-to-be's." I am *supposed to be* logical, capable, and imaginative. Do we feel like we are always falling short of these internal goals? Or do we see that we ignore some values or give them too little importance in ways that have a negative impact on us?

Mary's results showed her part of the reason she wasn't a good Home School President: the social and competence values aren't highest in her orientation, and she tended to overlook their importance. She also didn't give enough time to the planning and administrative details that make an association run. This shows her where she needs to put more effort. In her work as a professor, she consciously makes herself plan out the semester ahead of time. She still makes mistakes on details, but she found this is a good habit that now makes her life easier and helps her enjoy teaching.

Life Goals

With an idea of your talents and values, it is time to examine the goals you have for your life. Before you think about your specific life goals compare the following quotes:

> I don't know about you, but I want everything. I don't want any contradictions or forced choices. I want to eat and drink all I like and never gain weight. I want the freedom and flexibility of a single life and all the rewards of a loving spouse and children. I want to live in a small, intimate, low-pressure academic town and have all the challenges, money, and status of a job that may only be available in places like New York or Chicago. I want Santa Claus to come along and let me have it all. And I don't think I am unusual in this. I think most people, reasonable or not, want just about everything.[3]

> And God our Father gave us the task of protecting the earth—not for money, but for ourselves: for men and women. We have this task! Nevertheless men and women are sacrificed to the idols of profit and consumption: it is the "culture of waste." If a computer breaks it is a tragedy, but poverty, the needs and dramas of so many people end up being considered normal. . . . This "culture of waste" tends to become a common mentality that infects everyone. Human life, the person, are no longer seen as a primary value to be

respected and safeguarded, especially if they are poor or disabled, if they are not yet useful—like the unborn child—or are no longer of any use—like the elderly person.[4]

These two quotes embody what St. Paul was getting at when he wrote: "For those who live according to the flesh set their minds on the things of the flesh, but those who live according to the Spirit set their minds on the things of the Spirit" (Rom 8:5). As human beings we want it all, as Christians we need to develop a new perspective. With that in mind, the next exercise asks you to consider your goals in several areas: spiritual growth and practice of the faith, personal relationships, career satisfaction, community participation, learning and education, leisure satisfactions, status and respect, and material reward and possessions. This sequence was chosen deliberately to prioritize the main components of your vocation: God, relationships, work and community participation. Status and material rewards come last, since they are the biggest challenge for Christians when we decide to fully live our faith.

Exercise 9: Identifying my goals

In each of the areas, fill in your goals, adding personal reflections as you wish. The first and most important goal is spiritual growth.

Spiritual Growth and Practice of the Faith
Our goal is heaven, the realized kingdom of God. As the Baltimore Catechism puts it, God made us to know, love, and serve God in this life and be happy with him forever in the next. What goals do you have for your spiritual life and faith? Is it more regular prayer times? More participation in your faith community?
Specific Goals
1.
2.
3.

Personal Relationships

Family, friends, coworkers, and neighbors are all part of our network. What relationships are most important in your life, and how do you want them to develop over time?

Specific Goals

1.

2.

3.

Career Satisfaction

What do you want to achieve in your career? Note that there is a separate goal for material rewards, such as salary, below.

Specific Goals

1.

2.

3.

Community Participation

This includes your activities with civic, political, and charitable organizations, as well as community groups such as neighborhood watch and local sports leagues. What do you want to do to participate in your community?

Specific Goals

1.

2.

3.

Learning and Education

This can be formal or informal education, self-improvement classes, continuing education for career advancement, or even the development of skills and knowledge for hobbies. How do you want to be a lifelong learner?

Specific Goals

1.

2.

3.

Leisure Satisfactions

This includes what you do now and what you would like to do at some point in the future. What activities help you de-stress? What have you wanted to do but haven't had a chance to try?

Specific Goals

1.

2.

3.

Status and Respect

What counts for you as respect? Where do you wish to have status or acknowledgement of your contributions?

Specific Goals

1.

2.

3.

Material Rewards and Possessions
What income level are you aiming for—wealth, comfort, security, voluntary simplicity, or evangelical poverty? What possessions do you want?
Specific Goals
1.
2.
3.

Exercise 10: Setting priorities

You have written your goals in eight categories. Look over the list of goals and select the goals that you consider most important, choosing no more than 8. You may take them from any category; you don't need to have one from each. Rank them in terms of importance (1 is most important).

Exercise 11: Anticipating conflicts

Look over your goals and identify potential conflicts. For example, a college student had the goals of becoming a neurosurgeon and of being a good mother. She recognized that these goals might conflict during her training. When she was qualified and in practice, she would have more control over her schedule. The point of the exercise is not to tell you what choice to make, but to bring out the conflicts so that you can make good decisions. List the conflicts between your goals in order of importance.

Getting Outside of Your Own Head

The next exercise is to identify a mentor in your life and arrange an interview with him or her. The mentor may be someone you admire, even though you don't know the person very well, or it can be someone whom you know well and who knows you well, such as a relative, pastor, or spiritual director. When I teach my course on vocation, I invite people to come and talk to the class. I have used these questions to get them to tell their story. The experience is really rewarding not only for the students but also for the people telling their story. They seem to see things in a different light when others value them and their gifts.

Exercise 12: Mentor interview

Choose a mentor and arrange a meeting with plenty of time for a wide-ranging conversation. The following questions are a guide, but feel free to pursue any interesting lines of thought you or your mentor may have.

1. How did you discover your talents?
2. Did you have a mentor/guide to help you?
3. How do your values influence your vocation as a spouse, parent, or citizen, and in your work?
4. How did you develop your gifts in your career?
5. How do you integrate all aspects of your life?
6. How does your Christian faith provide a focus for your life?
7. If you have chosen someone who knows you well, ask what he or she would identify as your talents.

After the interview, prepare a summary. Think about the similarities and differences between your mentor and yourself. What can you learn from the mentor? What in your life has been affirmed by the interview?

Stages of Life

Where we are in life, just starting life as an adult or nearing our death, influences how we think about our goals and talents and our vocation. My father felt lost when he was forced to retire from his job. Fortunately, he was involved in the church and town, and over time he began to build an active life that included caring for his grandchildren.

I divide our life into four stages: formation, exploration, maturity, and contemplation. The lines between these stages generally could be marked as childhood, young adulthood, adulthood, and senior years. *Formation* is the stage where habits are formed and an outlook created. Our "work" is getting an education and learning to become independent and contributing members of the family and community. We are initiated into the faith that we were granted in our baptism, through religious education and reception of the sacraments. Children are not just the recipients of grace, however. They should see themselves as important disciples (as *Apostolicam Actuositatem* reminds us).

Exploration is the stage when we are willing to test the boundaries and move beyond our comfort zone. We are forced into this when we move from childhood into adulthood. We are stepping from the security of childhood and family into the unknown and feel an inner turmoil. This is the usual stage for a major decision about what Catholics call the "state of life": am I called to love God as a layperson, married or single, or as a priest or religious? This is also the time when many Catholics stop practicing the faith because they do not see how it is relevant to the problems they see in the world around them. In psychological research about religion, this stage is a transition from adolescence, when all authority-centered knowledge is challenged, to a personal, mature faith that understands that there are many possible ways to live and that one's faith life must be authentic and freely chosen.[5]

Maturity is the stage of commitment. We are now keeping our needs and those of others in balance, as we are involved in jobs, family, and community. This may be the busiest stage of life, when things can easily get overwhelming. We have so many obligations that we almost lose ourselves in our tasks. It is crucial to take time to examine what we are doing and why, rather than simply going along with things as they are.

Finally, *contemplation* is the time of completion when we can look over the whole of our life and see God's love. Aging can be a time of developing wisdom and peace, or a frenetic search for our lost youth. We are closer to death. Our friends are dying, doctors appear as young as high school students, and we are reminded of our mortality each time we look in the mirror. We are freed from many obligations, but not from our needs for connecting with others and being of service. Seeing retirement as a long search for pleasure without struggle or responsibilities toward others is not a healthy viewpoint.

Exercise 13: Life stages

Use the following matrix to think about your life under the four areas by the stage of life. I have inserted approximate ages, but feel free to ignore them if you wish. Think back over your childhood experiences, friendships made at college or in young adulthood, first work experiences, and so on—all of these help us to discover who we are and decide who we want to be. List key experiences or relationships that have influenced your view of yourself and your calling. If you haven't reached one or more of these stages, this is the time to do some dreaming. Consider how you see your life developing. What obligations do you have now, and will they change in the next stage of life? When you are in your 80s, what will you want to have done with your life? Assuming you are still healthy, what will you be doing in each of these areas? Maybe you are in the maturity stage and are fully occupied with work and family. You want to do more to help others, but right now your schedule is full. Pencil in a volunteer service as a part of your contemplation stage.

As Christians we do not start with a blank slate and say that we want to be rich and famous. Our primary goal is union with God: loving God and being loved by God without the barrier of sin. This is the overall goal for our life, and so we must judge all our other goals in light of it. We are no longer free to think only of ourselves. Our God is a trinitarian God, a communion of persons. We bear the image of God in our relatedness to others. We need to ask ourselves whether our career ambitions conflict with this goal: do we give enough time to the people in our lives, or do we expect them to wait until we have accumulated enough money and only *then* will we have time for them?

Life Stage	Talents	Areas of living your vocation			
		Work	*Relationships*	*Civic Community*	*Spiritual Community*
Formation 0–18					
Exploration 18–35					
Maturity 35–70					
Contemplation 70+					

Catholic Social Teaching

As laypeople in the world, we will be participating in the economy and politics, the social life of our time. It is not enough to be a good person who doesn't tell lies and is kind to others. We need to reform our society and think of ourselves within the larger community. For Americans, with our history of rugged individualism, this can be difficult. Maybe an example will make it clearer: we would never think of shoplifting a pair of jeans, but can we see that buying a new pair of jeans that are made in a sweatshop for 10 dollars is tantamount to stealing someone's wages? When we saw the news footage about the fire at the Bangladesh clothing factory, did we connect that with the bargains we love to buy? Do we take time to find out where the stuff we buy comes from?

Catholic Social Teaching is the name for the popes' teaching on the morality of living in community and dealing with the big ethical questions that come up when we are involved in the complex issues of economics, politics, and international relations. Through its social teaching the church has given us principles by which to judge actions and society—principles based on the fundamental teaching of *human dignity*. This is the notion that each and every person counts—the young, old, disabled, and sick as much as the fit, strong, healthy, and handsome. Each person is God's creation and precious in God's sight. This is the foundation for the other principles: *solidarity*—that is, the notion that we are all equally valuable and a part of one another. What happens to children in sweatshops in Asia matters to each of us, and we cannot just turn a blind eye. Therefore we seek the *common good*, which is not just the sum of everyone's desires, like a great buffet dinner with ribs and chicken and vegetarian options. It is the good for everyone and for *each* one. This means that anything that is harmful to one segment of the population (pornography, for instance) is not part of the common good, even if lots of people want it. Equally, it is not right that only some people have the means to live while others struggle on the edge of subsistence. Seeking the common good means that we need to pay special attention to the least, the poorest, and ensure that they are not excluded from community and are supplied with their needs. This is the *preferential option for the poor*. Because we all have dignity and gifts to offer, we are all called to *participate* in society; we don't get a pass because we don't like the problems of dealing with other people. We not only have to give money to the charities that relieve hunger, but we have to participate and vote in a way that will lessen the causes of hunger. To encourage and foster participation, the final principle, *subsidiarity*, insists that decisions should be made by those most affected wherever possible. The neighborhood should work on the neighborhood's problems first and only appeal to the city, state, and federal government when necessary. Equally, the higher levels of authority should respect the freedom and autonomy of the lower levels. These six principles guide our choices as members of a society trying to build justice and peace.

We develop our talents and the gifts of the Spirit in our own life and in our relationships with others. To check whether we are on the right path as Christians, answering the call to holiness and rightly ordering the secular world for justice and peace, we can test our goals by evaluating how they fit with the principles of Catholic Social Teaching.

Exercise 14: Evaluating our goals

Look over the principles below. They are one axis of the next matrix. Enter your goals from exercise 9 in the first column and test them against the principles of Catholic Social Teaching. Use the following symbols: a plus-sign (+) for helpful impact, a minus sign (–) for negative impact, and a zero (0) for no impact. Evaluate each of them by these definitions of the principles of Catholic Social Teaching.

Human Dignity: the image of God in every human—no matter how young, small, old, sick, or frail—respected by virtue of his or her creation and called to be in communion with other human beings and with God (CCC 357).

Solidarity: the equality of all in dignity and rights and the common path of individuals and peoples toward an ever-more committed unity (*Compendium of the Social Doctrine of the Church* [hereafter CSD] 192).

Subsidiarity: showing concern for the family, groups, associations, local territorial realities; in short, for that aggregate of economic, social, cultural, sports-oriented, recreational, professional, and political expressions to which people spontaneously give life and which make it possible for them to achieve effective social growth (CSD 185).

Common Good: the good of each person and of society together (CSD 164).

Participation: the duty to participate, as an individual or in association with others, in the cultural, economic, political, and social life of the community.

Preferential Option for the Poor: duty to make those whose living conditions interfere with their proper growth the focus of particular concern (CSD 182).

	Human Dignity	Solidarity	Subsidiarity	Common Good	Participation	Preferential Option for the Poor
Goal 1						
Goal 2						
Goal 3						
Goal 4						
Goal 5						
Goal 6						
Goal 7						
Goal 8						

Did this exercise make you rethink your goals? Do you find that the principles of Catholic Social Teaching help you to reorganize your priorities? We are called by God as persons within a community, and Catholic Social Teaching gives us a practical way to identify how we are contributing to the building up of that community.

Conclusion

We are made in the image of God as unique individuals who are by nature relational. We are called to love God and love others. That love is expressed in our daily work, our relationships, our community life, and our parish life. By doing these exercises I hope you have a better idea of how you are already living your vocation as a Christian, making Christ known and working to build a world of justice and peace. By working through these exercises, I hope you will have a clearer idea of where God is calling you to be a disciple. Maybe you will be pursuing new volunteer opportunities; maybe you have a new conception of the work you are already doing. It is important to come back to these exercises from time to time with a friend, mentor, or spiritual director to check that you are following God's call for your particular life.

Wherever God calls us to be, in our state of life and our particular circumstance, we have to live in a way that follows St. Francis's admonition: "Preach always, and if necessary use words." Our witness of life is the most important witness we give. In chapter 5 we will look at some ways to do that through the practices of humility, stewardship, and a life lived in balance.

chapter 5

Living a 24/7 Christian Life

The exercises in the last chapter should have helped us identify what nature has given us to use in our vocation. Our abilities and talents are the raw material that God's grace will build upon for us to do our part in rightly ordering the secular sphere as the fathers of the Second Vatican Council asked. That task has many parts: work, family, community, and the parish. In this chapter we look at how to live the universal call to holiness. For laypeople living out our vocation in the secular world, the holiness we seek is primarily the holiness of unity of life. Our life—whether in the workplace, the home, or in the privacy of the bedroom—must have the integrity of which the Beatitudes speak: we are pure of heart as we seek God through our life and work in the world. One description of this unity and integrity is that we are the same person and act the same way whether we are in public, with our friends or family, or alone in our bedroom. In other words, we are the same person in private and in public.

This integrity is the basis for the Christian witness of life. All of us observe each other; people are fascinating. If we are known as Christians people will observe what we do and say and compare it to what we say we believe. How we live day to day, in all the areas of our life, is as important a witness as choosing the right career or volunteer work. It is not good to be a crabby volunteer at the homeless shelter; our attitude can negate our good actions.

Three principles from Benedictine spirituality will help us advance in this quest for holiness and in our lives as disciples. They are humility, stewardship, and a life lived in balance. These principles provide a framework for living out our vocation 24/7. They are the basis for the witness that speaks louder than any words. These principles come from the *Rule of St. Benedict*, a document that goes back some 1,500 years and is the basis for the Benedictine monastic communities around the world. The Rule is very short and may be read in one sitting. Benedictines read part of it every day. You may wonder how such an old document designed to set up a monastic community may have relevance to a layperson in the twenty-first century. The answer is that St. Benedict knew the human heart inside and out. His Rule gives us a guide for seeking God in our daily life.

Benedict knew the importance of work in life. Many people know the Benedictine motto: *ora et labora* (pray and work). Prayer is the source of our strength, the development of our friendship with God. It is the foundation and support for our vocation. Prayer is not an optional extra if we are serious about living as a true disciple. We give our time to those we love, so we must set aside time to be with the Lord. Benedict arranged prayer so that the monks were constantly reminded that everything depends on God. They prayed literally morning, noon, and night—seven times a day, plus once in the middle of the night. Prayer is the point of being a monk then and now.

Saint Benedict balanced the times of prayer with times of work. He required his monks to do manual labor in an age when most work was done by slaves. His Rule creates a community bound by mutual service, first in prayer and then in work, to supply the necessities for the community and guests, especially the poor who come to the monastery. To keep the community functioning he emphasizes humility in each member and requires good stewardship of the monastery's goods. He sets up a pattern of life that balances the need to work, pray, and rest.

The Benedictine principles act as guidelines for living a disciple's life. They guide us in the path of holiness and help unite our spiritual and daily lives. Humility may be one of the hardest practices for us to accept, so we shall start by looking at St. Benedict's 12-step program, otherwise known as chapter 7 of the Rule, titled "Humility."

Humility

The modern world may not value humility, but it surely hates the opposite, pride or self-importance. In fact there is a new word for people being falsely humble: the *humblebrag*. "So stressed, no social life with my new business going so well!" There are Twitter sites devoted to collecting these from celebrities such as this one from Stephen Fry: "Oh dear. Don't know what to do at the airport. Huge crowd, but I'll miss my plane if I stop and do photos . . . oh dear don't want to disappoint."[1] One of the latest forms of the humblebrag uses the word "blessed" as in, "So blessed to have this exciting new relationship!"

Bragging is not a new phenomenon. We all dread the Christmas letter season when we hear from our faraway friends whose children are one step away from an Olympic gold medal and the Nobel Peace Prize. Bragging about the children has become so common and obnoxious that *The New York Times* social-advice columnist recommends that parents who want to keep their friends acknowledge that their children have flaws as well as accomplishments.

We live in a media world of celebrity where people compete to be the best known, the most important, and to have the Twitter account with the most followers. Magazines alternatively praise and mock those whom they "celebrate." And some of the celebrities believe their own publicists. We identify those people by the phrase that turns a celebrity (or anyone who uses it) into a figure of mockery: "Do you know who I am?"

Our world has recognized the problem of pride and self-conceit, and knows how much it harms relationships. It just isn't sure what to do about it. Gurus tell business people to show up on time and pay attention to those around them. Most advice comes down to remembering that we aren't the only persons in the world.

The gospel writers identify the source of our problem: our hearts. From the fullness of the heart the mouth speaks. Our hearts are wounded by original sin. We are each inclined to think we are the only person in the world. At the same time we think we have to earn love; we have to wear status symbols so that people know we are important. We think we need the external signs because we are afraid that others will find out that we aren't as wonderful as we try to pretend we are. We can even think this way about God and his love for us. We think we have to go to church so God knows we are good people. We learn our faith as children, and children sometimes understand faith in God as a bargain: "I must be good and then God will take care of me." Many of us never grow out of that primitive idea of religion. We need a change of heart, and then what we do and say will start to change too.

Fortunately, we have a living, breathing example of humility to guide us—Pope Francis. Look at his choices: the name Francis, the black shoes, paying his hotel bill himself, calling the newspaper vendor in Argentina to cancel his subscription, his introduction of himself as the Bishop of Rome. All of these tell us that he views everyone as his brother and sister, that even though he holds an extremely important office he doesn't think that makes him better or more important than other people. When he is asked who he is, he replies, "I am a sinner."

This has caused a media storm known as "the Francis effect." *The Economist* editorial talks about the pope's skills as a turnaround CEO. The Francis effect will be lasting because Pope Francis is a truly humble man who is also a servant leader. We would do very well to imitate him, beginning with getting our heart right.

Humility above anything else is truthfulness about ourselves. I am a sinner. All of us start with the truth that we are God's creatures, dependent upon God for everything, loved by God even though we are sinners, and made by God to be in relationship with others. This can be hard for us to accept, especially if we are talented and well educated. We can be pretty successful at most things in our life through our own efforts. But if we bring that attitude into our faith it will kill us. Look at the people in the gospels. The successful, religious people, the Pharisees, could not accept Jesus and his message of repentance. The people who knew they were sinners, the prostitutes and tax collectors, heard Jesus with gladness and believed him. We each need to see ourselves as sinners whom God knows intimately and loves beyond measure—then the Gospel will be good news for us.

When we see things in the light of truth we realize that all is gift: our life, our talents, our family, and our goods. God pours his love over us in countless ways, but we need to have the eyes to see it. When our self-worth is grounded on God's love for us, we can see our accomplishments as our gift back to God. As we pray and meditate on God's Word, we realize that God is superabundant love and an everlasting fountain of good things. We no longer see love as a zero-sum game that requires God to love someone else less if he loves us more. This frees us, sinners though we know ourselves to be, to see the face of Christ in everyone we meet and God's hand in the creation that surrounds us. Instead of seeing ourselves as masters of the universe, we see ourselves as the servants of all, as Christ told us to be at the Last Supper.

To help us change our hearts and get away from the pride that makes us so unhappy, we can follow Benedict. He writes of humility as a ladder of twelve steps, each one depending on the one before. The first four steps dethrone the ego from the center of the universe:

Step 1: "A man keeps the *fear of God* always *before his eyes* (Ps 36:2)" (RB 7.10).

Step 2: "A man loves not his own will nor takes pleasure in the satisfaction of his desires; rather he shall imitate by his actions that saying of the Lord: *I have come not to do my own will, but the will of him who sent me* (John 6:38)." (RB 7.31-32).

Step 3: "A man submits to his superior in all obedience for the love of God" (RB 7.34).

Step 4: "In this obedience under difficult, unfavorable or even unjust conditions, his heart quietly embraces suffering and endures it without weakening or seeking escape" (RB 7.35-36).

Fear of the Lord is not a cowering before an angry God, but rather it is the proper respect for the goodness of God. We have forgotten that goodness can be terrifying. Whenever angels show up in the Bible, their first words are "Do not be afraid." The first step acknowledges God as God and that we, his creatures, are dependent upon his goodness for everything.

In steps 2 and 3, we see the monk give up his right to please himself. Benedict's rules have the monks give up their autonomy, their authority to say what they will do and when. As laity we have autonomy, the freedom to control our own time in some measure. This is a particular difficulty for me; I am committed to my agenda and irritated by interruptions. C. S. Lewis described the root of this problem in *The Screwtape Letters*, where he writes that one of the best ways the devil has of tempting us to sin is the assumption that "my time is my own." Lewis writes: "He [the Christian] is also, in theory committed to a total service of the Enemy [Christ]; and if the Enemy appeared to him in bodily form and demanded that total service for even one day, he would not refuse. . . . Now if he thinks about his assumption for a moment, even he is bound to realize that he is actually in this situation every day."[2] A spiritual director helped me to see that the constant interruptions that were my life as a stay-at-home mom were exactly where Christ was calling me. It is a good thing to plan your day, but not set that plan in stone. We need to freely give to those who ask us to help them.

The assumption that we own our time has the corollary that we believe that we are owed a pleasant life. It is a struggle to accept illness, disability, or the loss of a job. It isn't easy at all. But we make it harder on ourselves when we have the habit of thinking that we are in charge of everything and that everything should go our way. How often do we hear Christians complaining when they suffer illness or loss? Yet we follow the one man who never sinned and was brutally put to death. That should teach us that life isn't fair.

We need to learn to accept things in our hearts, the source of our thoughts, words, and actions, so that when we are faced with suffering we can bear it patiently. Step 4 requires that we build this habit by giving up the inner grumbling. I learned not to bite the head off someone who asked for my help at an inconvenient time. Sadly, though, in my heart I am usually either seething quietly or, worse yet, preening about what a good Christian I am. Neither attitude is life-giving because the focus is still on me. The outer action and the inner thoughts are in opposition rather than unity. Benedict hated this kind of hypocrisy. He wants his followers to have a pure heart that truly seeks God and loves the neighbor.

Step 5, "A man does not conceal from his abbot any sinful thoughts . . . but confesses them humbly" (RB 7.44), is a call for radical honesty. Anyone who has tried to live the first steps of humility will have rebellious and sinful thoughts. It is only when we try to be good that we start to really want to rebel. Have you noticed that on most days you might live without snacking between meals at all—but on Ash Wednesday, when no between meal eating is the rule, you crave snacks? We are marked by a propensity to sin, and concealment gives sin power. How much better would the church be now if instead of hiding and concealing the problems with sexual abuse it had honestly confronted and dealt with them? We need to be honest about ourselves with ourselves, our spouse and children, and our spiritual director. Other people experience the darkness we carry—if you're feeling brave, ask your children or your spouse what you should work on during Lent. When we acknowledge our faults honestly, we can repent and begin to repair the relationships we have harmed.

Benedict's next steps are a direct challenge to our culture of self-esteem. For twenty-first-century Americans, convinced that we are special and raised in ways that value the individual over the group, these steps may help us return to a sensible balance between ourselves as individuals and ourselves as part of God's family.

Step 6: "A monk is content with the lowest and most menial treatment" (RB 7.49).

Step 7: "A man not only admits with his tongue but is also convinced in his heart that he is inferior to all and of less value" (RB 7.51).

Step 8: "A monk does only what is endorsed by the common rule" (RB 7.55).

These, especially step 7, sound rather unhealthy. And they are indeed unhealthy if we focus only on ourselves. But if we turn to God's greatness and love we come to see ourselves as lowly and unworthy and realize that all is gift. We are, at one and the same time, really special, a unique creation of God, and one of the many people in the human family. If we can see that in true perspective, then we will have taken the first and hardest step toward truly living out solidarity. We will be able to see ourselves as connected and loved by God as our brothers and sisters are loved, not more and not less.

The command to follow the common rule strikes at the spirit of competition that feeds our pride. Do we really want to be one of the crowd, or do we want to be the special one? We want to be not just successful, but a little more successful than our rival. It is okay to want to use your talents to excel, but it is definitely *not* okay to want to use them so others know you're better than they are. This is one of the tests that can tell us when we are being driven by pride, and if we are, we need to repent and try again.

Now that Benedict has sorted out our thinking, showing us our place in God's creation, he turns to our speech:

Step 9: "A monk controls his tongue and remains silent" (RB 7.56).

Step 10: "He is not given to ready laughter" (RB 7.59).

Step 11: "A monk speaks gently and without laughter, seriously and with becoming modesty" (RB 7 60).

Benedict is very concerned with what we say. He has numerous prohibitions of grumbling, and he is not a big fan of laughter. To appreciate his wisdom, look at C. S. Lewis's four kinds of laughter: "Joy, Fun, the Joke Proper and Flippancy."[3] Joy is the laughter that arises from the heart when we are truly happy. Fun is the expression of our instinct to play. The Joke Proper arises from the sudden perception of incongruity. Jokes can help us see things in true proportion and can be good, or they can be vehicles for malice, sarcasm, and put-downs. Flippancy is mockery of serious subjects. We see so much of this in our culture, and it makes speaking of virtue difficult. Benedict wants us to be charitable in our speech, gentle, and modest. He wants us to have hearts that are loving, and he wants our words to speak truly from that heart.

Finally, **Step 12** dictates that "a monk always manifest humility in his bearing no less than in his heart" (RB 7.62). This is the goal that we become persons of integrity; that our inner and outer lives match. We act humbly because we are truly humble. Instead of pretending to be humble while the little voice inside cries, "Look at me! Look at me!" we take our place as a beloved child of God in his human family, thinking of others and not ourselves.

Humility helps us in all four areas of our vocation. In the family it helps us to appreciate each other and realize that we depend on and contribute to one another. Humility means we value each other for our existence, not for our accomplishments. We don't have to be perfect to be loved. When our families model this, they will be living out the best sort of domestic church, where all are welcomed, accepted, loved, and forgiven. Parents should be the models of servant leadership and train their children to work for the good of the family, not just of themselves. When those children grow up, parents need to step back and trust their now adult children to handle their lives. Humility makes the space for love to flourish in the family.

In our workplace it is harder to see humility as a virtue. It is often confused with being a doormat and letting others take credit for our work. That is not what it means, since humility is truth. It means that everyone, from the executive vice president to the janitor, is part of the team that gets things done. It means owning up to failures. It means going against the culture of many workplaces, where the office politics breed a climate of fear, suspicion, and backbiting. No one can thrive in such an environment. No individual can change the entire culture of an organization, but each of us can refuse to play the games, abstain from the backbiting, and get on with the job.

This is truly revolutionary and has real impact in the world. A well-known business researcher, Jim Collins, wrote about humility in the *Harvard Business Review,* naming it as one of the defining characteristics of a Level 5 leader.[4] He describes the difference between Level 4 and Level 5 leaders with an analogy of the mirror and the window. When you ask Level 4 leaders about their success they speak of their own talents and dedication and insight (the mirror). When you ask them about problems, they talk about their team members not being up to the job, or about the bad economy (the window). Level 5 leaders, on the other hand, attribute their success to the people around them (the window) and any failures to themselves (the mirror). This kind of leadership arises from deep within the heart; it isn't a technique learned in a workshop and tried out for a quick fix.

In the neighborhood, humility reminds us of the importance of everyone in our community and should jolt us out of our complacency when our brothers and sisters are in want, taken advantage of, and pushed to the margins. When we vote, we need to vote not for our self-interest, but for the common good, with special attention to the needs of those who are poor. When we volunteer, we need to remember that the people we serve are also serving us. When we run the youth sports teams, we can build this kind of healthy humility which recognizes players' strengths and weaknesses and encourages them to work together for the best results.

In our faith community, we should be reminded of the humility of Christ, who put himself into our hands so that we could kill him. Parishes, like all human communities, suffer from our egos and our need to compete with others. Yet it is here that we should become what we pray. When we confess our sins at the beginning of Mass, we should truly repent. When we pass the peace, we should be turning into true peacemakers. We should come out of Sunday Mass reminded that we are loved by God and empowered by the Spirit to go into the world and love it the way Jesus did. We will know we are making progress when we let someone cut in front of us in the parking lot without getting angry.

Humility can help alleviate much of the financial pressure we are under. As laity in the world, we must provide for our needs and take prudent decisions not to become a burden on others. But we are not called to spend our money on bigger houses, newer cars, and more and more stuff to prove how successful we are. Humility can free us from needing the status symbols, which means that we can live the next principle—stewardship.

Stewardship

In chapter 1 we looked at consumerism, the idea that we can buy our way to happiness. The world is waking up to the problems with that lifestyle and is trying to make some changes. Many Catholics have given up fasting on Friday, but now environmentalists encourage meatless Mondays. A sharing economy of bartering and handing on goods has been developing alongside other consumer pressures to increase buying. Decluttering and getting rid of our stuff are featured in almost every design or household magazine, and we build storage facilities where we pay to have a climate-controlled place for the stuff that doesn't fit into our homes but we can't bring ourselves to give up. We are far from our frugal ancestors' creed of use it up, wear it out, and make it do or do without. That phrase has become a rallying cry for the new movement of thoughtful consumption and frugality. CAFOD (Catholic Agency for Overseas Development) has an even better way of expressing it: live simply so that others may simply live.

Living a lifestyle of simplicity was the mark of the early Christians and monastic communities. In the Acts of the Apostles, we have accounts of the early Christian community living a communal lifestyle where the rich would sell what they have to support the poor. Of course divisions arose (human nature never changes), and not everyone could live this way. When Christianity became the established religion of the empire, Christians wanting to live a more demanding Christian life withdrew into the desert or mountains and began monastic communities. Saint Benedict wanted to follow the practice of the early church, depending on God and each other for necessities and curbing the desire for goods. Benedictine monks live in a community that supplies them with their clothes, their tools for work, their food, and their shelter. In return no monk may have any personal possessions (RB 33).

We cannot just live Benedict's rule as laypeople in the world, since owning goods is part of our vocation. We must care for ourselves and those who depend on us, so we may adapt the Rule to our situation. We do this through stewardship—the practice of rightly valuing goods. Stewards were the servants of landowners who managed the property for their employers. Being a good steward means we recognize that we are caretakers, not owners. Stewardship starts from the same truth as humility: everything we have is a gift from God. And that means that everything is meant for all God's children, not just everyone alive now, but future generations too. We cannot take more than our share and not pay a price in our character. Original sin means we are naturally selfish, and we need to find ways to curb that tendency and develop our capacity to love others and live in solidarity.

Benedict was a realist. He understood that human beings need clothing and tools, books and art. In his Rule, Benedict recognized that the monks would have different needs, and he arranged for them to get what they needed. If they were working especially hard, they got extra food. If it was a cold climate, they had extra clothing and blankets. Some monks need more than others. So today a monk who needs special shoes gets them. He is admonished, however, to remember that "whoever needs more should feel humble because of his weakness, not self-important because of the kindness shown him" (RB 34.4). Benedict even understood the importance of keeping up appearances: if monks are sent on a journey they are given slightly newer and better-looking habits, but when they come home, it is back to the regular ones. Benedict also has rules to keep a running inventory of the goods of the monastery and rules for ensuring that everyone has the tools he needs and is responsible for caring for them. He gives us a good model for a household economy.

The goods of the monastery are in the charge of a cellarer, someone who is "wise, mature in conduct, temperate, not an excessive eater, not proud, excitable, offensive, dilatory or wasteful, but God-fearing" (RB 31.1-2). He is in charge of the temporal goods and must keep track of them and use them to meet the needs for the monks, the sick, the children, and the poor. "He will regard all utensils and goods of the monastery as sacred vessels of the altar" (RB 31.10). Here is a central principle of stewardship that we need today: goods are not something that we should use and discard without thought. We need to treat things with respect as they are part of God's good material creation.

The attitude that the things we need should be of good quality and be cared for carefully is the essence of stewardship that we can apply to our lives. We stop living a disposable lifestyle and begin to live and consume mindfully. We have to be our own cellarer and manage our household inventory. We have to look at the goods we have and see what is excess and could be shared with others. Our family has moved across the Atlantic several times, and I am always embarrassed by how many trips to the thrift store I have to make before the move. Better managers than I use the changing of seasons to discard things that are not used and make room for new things that will be.

Stewardship doesn't mean being unfashionable or poorly dressed. It does mean, however, that thought is given to what is needed and quality goods are purchased and taken care of. It is the opposite of our quickly changing fashion culture and its impetus toward instant gratification. It means taking time to think through how to care for one's needs—even a simple one, like shoes for work. When my husband bought one pair and wore them every day, they wore out in three months. He then bought two pairs of shoes and wore them on alternate days. This meant that each pair of shoes lasted for a year. So over the year he saved buying two pairs of shoes. This is a simple example, but it goes directly against our culture that constantly tells us that more is better.

Stewardship thinks about our impact on the earth, how many resources we are using, and how we can cut down on waste. Do we need to put chemicals on our lawns that prevent dandelions but also damage the environment for bees, when we can cut the grass more frequently so the dandelions do not bloom and form seeds? Stewardship sees insulating our homes and turning the thermostats down (or up in warmer months) so that we do not consume excess energy. Stewardship attends to our obligation to future generations; when we see ourselves as part of a larger human family we want to make sure that the goods of the earth are shared.

Clearly, most of us will practice stewardship within our homes, and our family budget meetings are a good place to start. One of the key principles is that we are not just being penny-pinchers—we are making a choice to live a more mindful way. Pope Francis has told us, "Throwing away food is like stealing from the table of those who are poor and hungry."[5] We must realize that our choices have global consequences, and we must teach our children this too. The children will do what they see us do; so if we collect more and more stuff, we mustn't be surprised that *they* want more and more stuff too. Stewardship helps to raise children who are kind and aware of others' needs. And it has an added bonus: they will learn to appreciate the toys and games they *do* have.

Part of good stewardship is setting aside time and money to serve others. Many families practice tithing, setting aside one-tenth of their income for charities. We find it easier to do this if we have a separate bank account for charitable giving, which simplifies accounting for it at tax time. But the real benefit is the chance to make a difference and support those on the margins. Nothing makes you feel as rich as the ability to make a real difference to others. We must use our talents and gifts along with our money in whatever area we are called to serve. We cannot use donations to distance ourselves from others' pain—we need to give of ourselves *as well as* our wealth.

In the workplace, stewardship can be a business win. Many companies are trying to be more sustainable. Companies are always looking for ways to cut costs, and the energy you *don't* use is the cheapest energy going. We can support those efforts and ensure that our attitude at work is as responsible about consumption as our attitude at home. We can do teleconferences rather than business travel, and we can support efforts to be better corporate citizens in our communities. We can encourage our firms to think in terms of sustainability as a long-term goal, which enhances the bottom line.

In the community, we can find common ground with neighbors of other faiths (or of no faith) by working together for a sustainable community. Some say that it doesn't matter what we do: other countries will just burn tons of coal, so we might as well enjoy our luxuries while we can. If our motivation for being good stewards is to solve global warming, then that argument is valid. If, however, we are being good stewards because we recognize the rights of all humans, including future generations, then we should not use our resources extravagantly at any time—regardless of any positive or negative consequences. We should live simply because it is the right thing to do. As a group, Christians have a reputation for not caring about the environment. I believe that is an unwarranted slur, but we certainly haven't put our theology of creation or principle of human solidarity into practice in the world.

Our parish community can be a place where sustainability can be linked to catechesis on Creation and Christ's incarnation. We make the connection between doctrine and the solidarity between human beings, and practical action, to ensure that we are living out our faith in ways that witness to others of our love for God and neighbor. We have a community that could develop a sharing economy, and we can help each other avoid the pressures to overconsume. It is hard to be the only mother who refrains from hosting an extravaganza for the birthday party, but a parish mother's group that is committed to stewardship can support its members by focusing on people and not stuff.

Humility is necessary to show us that we don't need stuff to give us status. Stewardship guides us in managing what we do need, and it shows us how to shed the excess in our lives and open ourselves to real solidarity: the care of others. When we commit ourselves to living simply, we find that we can practice Benedict's third principle—a live lived in balance.

A Life Lived in Balance

Much of the current writing about vocation focuses on the choice of a job, and it presents "job" and "vocation" as interchangeable. Yet one's work often presents a great challenge to a life lived in balance. Workers are either in jobs that demand 60+ hours a week or are unable to find a full-time job for a decent rate of pay and so have to take two or more jobs to make ends meet. In such situations we have to take a clear look at our expenses and our goals and decide what is truly important. For those living on the edge, multiple jobs are necessary for survival. If we are not in that situation, we should be advocates for those who are.

Work is a key part of the Christian vocation. Ideally, work should be something one loves because it uses one's talents for a good purpose, and provides sufficient material reward to support personal and family life. But this book maintains that the Christian vocation is bigger than just a choice of work. The lay Christian is called to discipleship in all areas of life: the family and other personal relationships, work, community life, and parish life. To live as a disciple, then, we need to learn to balance these areas.

Humility and stewardship grant the freedom to do this. Controlling our desires means that we don't need an ever-growing income but should separate our wants from our needs. When we have our desires under control we can make time for rest, recreation, family, and community. A life lived in balance harmonizes our needs for people and solitude, abundance and fasting, work and rest. People come first, and we have time to develop our relationships. The church insists in her social teaching on the primacy of people over the economy—the economy is to function for people, rather than enslaving people to the economy. In other words, we need to use our time to build our communities, not just our bank balance.

Benedict knew the importance of balance in a well-lived life and wrote his Rule with that in mind. He prescribed daily manual labor for his monks, saying, "Idleness is the enemy of the soul. Therefore, the brothers should have specified periods for manual labor as well as for prayerful reading" (RB 48.1). The monk's day is divided by prayer, and the times between meals and communal prayer is given to work, reading, or rest (RB 48). Sundays are given over to reading, although brothers who are too indolent to study must be given some work (RB 48.22-23). Benedict's ideal schedule has a rhythm, a chance for the body and mind to change gears and be refreshed in order to undertake the next task.

This balance was in service of the community. For instance, Benedict has a chapter specifically about lateness at prayer or at meals. He thinks that it is vital that the community be together for prayers and meals. Indeed, those who leave a meal early are reproved in the same way that those who, through their own fault, come late to the meal or come late to community prayers (RB 43).

Benedict's community lived a life in balance in order to foster healthy communal relationships. This is a lesson that our own society needs. We find ourselves either with no work, or needing to work so many hours that our time for family, community, and parish are severely limited. We substitute "quality time" for actual time. Much of that quality time, though, is spent with one-half of our mind on the conversation and the other half checking our devices for the latest message. Recovering balance is of crucial importance to our own health and the health of our society.

Healthy relationships in families and in communities depend on time spent together. As scientists have studied our brain and the limbic system that controls our emotional system, the importance of physical presence with one another has emerged:

> In a relationship, one mind revises another; one heart changes its partner. This astounding legacy of our combined status as mammals and neural beings is limbic revision: the power to remodel the emotional parts of the people we love, as our Attractors activate certain limbic pathways, and the brains' inexorable memory mechanism reinforces them.
>
> Who we are and who we become depends, in part, on whom we love.
>
> . . . Because our minds seek one another through limbic resonance, because our physiologic rhythms answer to the call of limbic regulation, because we change another's brains through limbic revision—what we do inside relationships matters more than any other aspect of human life. . . . Some cultures encourage emotional health; others do not. Some, including modern America, promote activities and attitudes directly antithetical to fulfillment.[6]

The idea of limbic resonance is that we affect each other by being together. Our bodies are functioning at a level of which we are hardly aware. By simply sitting on the couch with someone, you will find that your breathing starts to synchronize. Making eye contact with another human may be fleeting, but it establishes a real connection. We like eye contact so much that advertisers use it to attract us: open your cupboards and see Uncle Ben and the Quaker Oats "Quaker man" looking back at you. Neuroscience tells us that we are programmed to want to be part of a group working together for a common goal. Theology tells us that we bear the image of a trinitarian God—that is, that we are made for relationship. We must understand how important bonding with people in our families and communities is to our own and society's health. We need to balance our lives to give time to our relationships outside of work, thus enabling our families and communities to become strong and connected.

As an absolute minimum, we need to recover the idea of Sabbath, a day of rest. This was a key idea of God's revelation in both the Old Testament and Christ's teaching. We know our Lord's criticism of those who turned the Sabbath into a set of rules; he said that the Sabbath is made for man, not man for the Sabbath. He ignored some of the customs surrounding the Sabbath that had attained the force of law and that had become burdensome, but he maintained an emphasis on the day of rest because he knows that we need a break from our work and toil. We need time to rest. Anne-Marie Slaughter writes about Jack Lew, the former White House Chief of Staff, who observed the Jewish Sabbath in the midst of the pressures of Washington to work incessantly. Although people respected Lew for the honoring of his religious commitment, she writes, "It is hard to imagine, however, that we would have the same response if a mother told us she was blocking out mid-Friday afternoon through the end of the day on Saturday, every week, to spend time with her children. I suspect this would be seen as unprofessional, an imposition of unnecessary costs on co-workers. In fact, of course, one of the great values of the Sabbath—whether Jewish or Christian—is precisely that it carves out a family oasis, with rituals and a mandatory setting-aside of work."[7]

This is a challenge in a society where even Catholic youth sports leagues arrange games and practices on Sundays. The weekend is as busy as the workweek, and we have so many chores and activities. We need to see that we ignore our need for rest and recreation at our peril; we need to *want* control over our schedule. It will take real effort to do this, and it might not happen on Sunday, given the demands of work for many people. But if we commit to making one day a week for reconnecting with ourselves, our families, and our God, we will have begun the journey to a life lived in balance.

In our family we discovered that if we were out more than two nights a week things started to fall apart. We had adequate childcare, but as parents we were missing time with the children that we all needed. Each of us made a commitment to accept no more than two evening engagements a week. So what did we do when we were home? Not much really—we were just there. Our presence—being in the same room with the kids even if we are all reading different books or paying attention to different things—had a different feel than our absence. In our marriage, too, we found that we needed extended time to just be together in each other's presence. Now I know that what we were experiencing was the presence or lack of limbic resonance.

When we read the gospels, the overwhelming impression about Jesus' interactions with people is that he was totally present to them. He really saw them, and he listened to them. This is the Christlike witness we must imitate in all of our relationships. When we are together we need to really be *there*, and not just on our devices. One of the most important ways of being together is the family meal. Some programs for troubled teens insist that the family commit to eating together at least three nights a week before they will accept the teenager into the program. Executives who value their families can find a way to be home for dinner, or the family can commit to sharing at least three meals together a week—even if one of them is breakfast.

Making the kinds of choices that will make a life lived in balance possible means that we will not be living like our neighbors. It will be a challenge to make the choice for time together instead of lavish vacations and spending sprees. But that time is key to our Christian witness to our children and to their friends. When our house is the place the kids and their friends gather and there are adults who care for them and pay attention to them, we are truly witnessing to Christ and his care for everyone.

At work we may be fighting a culture that identifies working late with dedication, rather than looking at actual results. How we negotiate that depends on the situation; clearly, employment is necessary to support the family. But we can define our performance by what is produced, the project completed, and the number of sales booked, instead of how many hours we spent in our office. We can make a choice for family over professional success. Culture is slow to change, and the business world is a very conservative place. But if we no longer accept the long-hour, corporate-first ideology, we can make a difference. Each family will have to negotiate and renegotiate as needs and demands of work change. The time together should help the family become part of the local community.

One of the benefits of having balance in our lives is having time to give to others, in order to rebuild the links of community that make life satisfying for everyone and not just for those blessed with happy marriages and good jobs. We may find ourselves living in an anonymous suburb without natural centers for gathering and suffering the sense that no community exists at all. Yet if we get involved in local events and volunteering to serve others, we will benefit ourselves as well as the whole community. Christians should be the first volunteers to serve, rather than those who hold themselves aloof. Sports leagues need coaches, libraries and schools need literacy volunteers, and the civic association needs bodies for the cleanup days. By taking an active part in community life, we are giving our witness of life in places where the clergy may never be welcomed or heard.

Finally, the parish needs our presence. We need to be at Sunday Mass, as others depend on our presence. The act of praying together as a community binds us together, helps those who are needy and cannot pray themselves, and reminds us that we are going to heaven as a team and not as isolated individuals. One of the financial aid counselors at my university asks the students whether they are going to Mass. When they answer that no, they can pray by themselves, she responds, "Well, you don't need to go to a party Saturday either, you can get a six pack and drink it in your room." They usually laugh and recognize the truth that some experiences need to be shared.

Our parishes need us to be involved to build a real Christian community that will have a communal witness. Parishes need help not just with the internal jobs, such as catechist, usher, and musician, but with the outreach programs and social justice ministries too. Working with others toward a common goal is one of the most satisfying ways to spend time. It is why you hear volunteers say that they receive much more than they give.

The vocation of the disciple requires that we work to make the world a just and loving place and that we prioritize people above things. Humility, stewardship, and a life lived in balance will help us to do this and provide a true witness of life. Living this way authentically, however, will be impossible without the power that makes discipleship possible—prayer.

chapter 6

Prayer

"First of all, every time you begin a good work, you must pray to him most earnestly to bring it to perfection" (RB Prol. 4). Benedict sought a balance between work and prayer in the lives of his monks. If we are going to be disciples who bear good fruit, we, too, need to be people of prayer. As laity we will have to adapt how we pray to our situation, and that will change throughout our life. But pray we must.

Dr. Andre Delbecq, a nationally known author and teacher of workplace spirituality, found that many high-performing executives, no matter what their religious affiliation, built time for meditation into their day. The common pattern was first thing in the morning, just before starting the workday, between meetings, at the end of the day before going home, and at night before falling asleep. This kind of mindfulness—stopping activity and taking stock—is practiced by Christians, Buddhists, Hindus, Jews, Jains, Muslims, and atheists. Meditation and mindfulness is of such interest now that *Time* magazine published a cover story on it.[1]

As Christians we have a rich tradition of prayer upon which to draw, beginning with the sacraments, where we pray in community as Christ's body, the church. Praying together is essential for us as disciples; we need others' prayers for us, and they need our prayers for them. Prayer is what binds us into the communion we share, but this communal prayer should be supplemented with individual prayer.

There are no hard and fast rules about prayer; pray as you can. It may be as simple as a morning prayer, offering the day's work to God, and an evening prayer of thanksgiving and contrition for the good and bad parts of the day. It can be a daily rosary. There are many resources that can help us find a prayer style that works. Suggested here are two ways of praying that are part of Benedictine spirituality—the Liturgy of the Hours, which Benedictines call the *opus dei,* or "work of God," and *lectio divina,* or "divine reading."

Liturgy of the Hours

Benedict organized the monks' day around communal prayer. He listed seven times of prayer during the day and one in the middle of the night (RB 16). The Rule with its times of prayer interrupts the monks' work and constantly reminds them that all is from God. Benedict laid out complete instructions for prayers at these times, ensuring that the community would pray the entire Psalter, all 150 psalms, during a single week. He closes his detailed instructions with this: "Above all else we urge that if anyone finds this distribution of the psalms unsatisfactory, he should arrange whatever he judges better, provided that the full complement of one hundred and fifty psalms is by all means carefully maintained every week" (RB 18.22-23). Benedict recognized that prayer had to suit the community's situation.

From this monastic practice and a similar pattern of daily communal prayers by the cathedral clergy, the Liturgy of the Hours (also called the Divine Office) developed. It is the official public prayer of the church that priests are required to pray every day. Each prayer time, called an Office, includes psalms, a Scripture reading and response, intercessions, and a closing prayer. The main offices are Morning Prayer and Evening Prayer, traditionally recognized as Lauds and Vespers. In traditional practice, a full day's prayer would include these, as well as the Office of Readings and prayers at mid-morning, noon, mid-afternoon, and night. The psalms are organized in a four-week cycle, while the readings, antiphons, and responses change with the liturgical seasons and celebrations of the saints.

Most laity would not be able to pray like this every day. We probably do not even desire to live our lives this way (otherwise one would do well to investigate a monastic vocation), but we can learn several valuable lessons from Benedict. We should remember God through the day, much as the executives whom DelBecq described do. Certainly, framing the day with morning and evening prayers provides the opportunity to express our gratitude and repent our faults. While we can do this using our own words, praying the Office has some benefits.

When we pray the Office, we are praising God in God's own words: the Psalms. God's words become our words as we pray the same psalms in the four-week cycle. The words are engraved on our heart and are there when we are faced with great joy or great sorrow. It also helps stop the "gimmes,"—that is, when our prayer, instead of being Adoration, Contrition, Thanksgiving, and Supplication (ACTS), consists entirely of supplication: gimme this, gimme that. Morning and Evening Prayer frame the day with the prayer of the whole church, and we do our part in praying for others as they pray for us.

Praying the Office takes us out of our isolated individualism and unites us with the whole church. As a mother at home with young children, praying the Office provided me with a way of reconnecting with the worldwide church. Later, when I was sitting by my dying mother's bedside, it was a great comfort to have prayers that put my grief into God's universal love. It is so easy to become caught up in our immediate problems that we lose a sense of proportion; we forget about those who are in need of our prayers as we try to get through the day. Praying the Office reminds us that we are part of the Body of Christ, all praying together across time and space.

The Office is such a rich resource that we may use different parts of it at different times in our life. The Office of Readings has selections from Scripture and a second reading by the church fathers, saints, or other voices of the tradition, chosen to complement each other. During Lent those readings on their own can be the basis for prayer. Night Prayer, or Compline, is one of the shortest offices and works even with younger children. When we lived in Connecticut, the Archdiocese of Hartford had a radio station (WJMJ) that broadcast Night Prayer from St. Joseph's Abbey at the time that we got the children ready for bed. Just before going to sleep it is good for a child to hear, "Visit this house we beseech thee, O Lord, and drive apart from it all snares of the enemy. Let your holy angels dwell herein and keep us in peace." It became the family prayer then and after, especially during times of worry.

There are two versions of the official Liturgy of the Hours: a single-volume titled *Christian Prayer* and the full four-volume *Liturgy of the Hours*. There are apps and websites that provide all the texts of the prayers of the day, as well as the Mass texts. Within the same longstanding tradition of praying the hours, there are monthly magazines, such as *Give Us This Day* and *Magnificat,* that offer readings and prayers for morning and evening, along with the Mass readings of the day and a meditation. And monastic communities continue to develop and publish daily prayer guides that incorporate all of the traditional hours, from Vigils through Compline.[2] Many parishes pray Morning Prayer before or after the daily Mass. Religious houses often publish the schedule of their prayer times and welcome visitors who wish to participate. The Office is a resource for the whole church, not just religious and priests. Praying it will enrich your participation in daily Mass and the Sunday Liturgy and sanctify time as you move through the liturgical year, celebrating the church's feasts and seasons. I am especially fond of reclaiming Advent as a proper liturgical season of preparation and then celebrating the Christmas season from December 25 until January 6 (even though Catholics in the U.S. celebrate Epiphany on the first Sunday after New Year's). We don't have to live on mall time; we can choose to live on God's time.

In addition to this communal prayer, Benedictine monastics practice individual meditation on Scripture—a practice known as *lectio divina.*

Lectio Divina

Lectio divina is the private prayer of the monk as he meditates on Scripture. He reads a Scripture passage and then pauses to listen in his heart for a word that God is bringing to his attention. He reads the passage again, pausing to meditate on what he has read. And he will read the passage a third time and go into a prayer of listening for God's still small voice.

The Benedictine tradition of praying over the Scriptures distinguishes various senses of Scripture that help us integrate our faith and our life. First is the literal sense which includes not only what the words mean but also what kind of writing it is. The literal sense of a myth is the truth it conveys, so the creation stories in Genesis are not scientific accounts of creation but stories that carry important truth—namely, that God created everything out of nothing. The literal sense does require that we understand what the words mean, and what they meant to the writer of the passage (insofar as we can tell). If we don't know these things, we can't hope to make good sense of the message. This work is done by scholars and commentators so that in a good study Bible or Bible commentary the reader will find notes for these kinds of explanations.

So when we read the myth of the Great Flood, it isn't a newspaper report of the first global warming crisis; it is a story of God's covenant to care for the earth and not destroy it by flood. But we also need to ask things like: What is a cubit? A cubit is the span from the elbow to either the wrist or the end of the middle finger, from 17 to 22 inches. Now we can figure out how big Noah's ark was: "This is how you are to make it: the length of the ark three hundred cubits, its width fifty cubits, and its height thirty cubits" (Gen 6:15).

The literal sense is the foundation for the spiritual senses. In the Exodus story we read about the manna in the desert. The manna was a white flaky substance, and scholars debate what natural substance it was and how it came to feed the Israelites for forty years. On the basis of that knowledge we move to the spiritual senses of the manna: (1) the allegorical sense relates the events to Christ, such that the manna in the desert in Exodus is a sign of the Eucharist in the gospels and the writings of St. Paul; (2) the moral sense relates to how we should act, such that the manna teaches us to rely on God for our needs day to day; and (3) the anagogical sense puts things into the perspective of God's final plan, such that the manna is a sign of the heavenly banquet. The Catechism quotes a medieval couplet:

> The Letter speaks of deeds, Allegory to faith;
> The Moral how to act; Anagogy our destiny. (CCC 118)[3]

These four senses of Scripture are present when we practice *lectio divina*, the meditative repeated reading of the text that Benedictines use. In *Sacred Reading: The Ancient Art of Lectio Divina*, Cistercian monk Michael Casey summarizes the Benedictine prayer of *lectio divina* and its relation to these four senses of Scripture:

The Four Moments of *Lectio Divina*			
Sense of Scripture	Human Faculty	Function	Prayer
Literal	Intellect	Understanding the text	*Lectio*
Christological [Allegory]	Memory	Contextualizing the meaning	*Meditatio*
Behavioral [Moral]	Conscience	Living the meaning	*Oratio*
Mystical [Anagogical]	Spirit	Meeting God in the text	*Contemplatio*

Source: Michael Casey, *Sacred Reading: The Ancient Art of Lectio Divina* (Liguori, MO: Triumph, 1995), 57.

Lectio divina takes practice. Like all prayer, it requires quieting the inward chatter in order to tune into God. I find that the framework of *lectio* and the four senses of Scripture give me something to hold onto when distractions arise. It is also good to remember that Benedict wanted his followers to memorize the Scriptures. He had them reading the passages aloud so that more of their senses were involved. If we approach our daily meditation on Scripture this way, we will let it seep into our hearts at the deepest level.

Reading and praying over Scripture is most important because it brings us into immediate contact with the living Word of God. If we are attentive, we can open our hearts to the message that God wants us to hear. This kind of listening is especially important when we are thinking or talking about vocation—God's call to us as individuals in a particular time and place.

For the lay Christian, trying to live as a disciple in the secular world, reading and praying with Scripture is food for the journey. In our prayer we bring out problems to God and lay open our lives for his saving touch. I have learned over the years that prayer is not like television; problems are not solved in 30 minutes. But repeated prayer changes our heart, and then our problems become less daunting. When the heart is changed, it becomes easier to act as Jesus would have us act.

Setting aside time each day for this kind of prayer may seem burdensome at the beginning. But if we are faithful to the practice, we find that we discover the darkness in ourselves—our sin is always before us. It is a real temptation to stop praying since it makes us uncomfortable. But this is exactly the time to keep going. There will be periods of dryness when it seems that we are praying into a black hole and that no one is listening. Often it is because we are trying to make God into an idol, fitting him into our limited conceptions rather than letting go of our own ideas. If we remain faithful to prayer, however, the dark periods are often periods of great growth that only later reveal themselves as such.

Prayer and the Cross

The dark periods of prayer and the times of suffering in our lives remind us that we follow a Lord who laid down his life for us even though we didn't deserve it. The challenge of the faith is that each of us must imitate Jesus' love in our lives. Clearly, given our tendency to selfishness and sin, there are going to be some real struggles and failures along the way.

As Christians we do not have to face that alone; as Catholics we have the blessing of the sacrament of reconciliation to meet Christ, in the person of the priest, for healing and guidance along the way. Many Catholics remember mandatory confession from their childhood and cannot imagine going back to rattling off a memorized list of sins. Fair enough—the sacrament should be more than an automatic grace dispenser. But the gift of this sacrament is there if we laity will only take advantage of it.

I find it helpful to have a regular confessor. I am very good at deceiving myself about my spiritual life, and having a confessor who has come to know me is a great help in unmasking these deceptions. Having another person's perspective and suggestions has really helped me to grow as a Christian. Hearing a human voice say that I am forgiven is more reassuring to me than simply praying alone in my room. All Christians can benefit from having a spiritual director or guide to help them make sense of their spiritual journey and hold them accountable for living authentically.

Our life is a journey back to God, and everything that is not of God must be purged. That is a real, lifelong struggle. Every time I think I have my ego beaten down, it pops up again, usually in an even worse form, such as spiritual pride. Having a regular confessor helps me keep a sense of proportion and keep my eyes on God, not myself. It is this that gives us the confidence to go on.

One of the sins I must confess most often is the neglect of prayer. There are days when it is all I can do to say an Our Father. But that is how Jesus taught us to pray, and it contains everything that we need to pray well. I have learned that I am a poor servant of Christ, yet he can use me anyway. There is a real liberation of the spirit when one faces oneself as a sinner and trusts in God's continued mercy and love.

Conclusion

Ultimately, prayer is our ongoing friendship with the Lord. He offers us his love, and we will benefit from that relationship, like all other relationships, when we make time for it. Prayer is the foundation for our life as disciples. By strengthening our relationship with

Christ, prayer gives us the cheerful confidence that we need to be effective disciples, in whatever particular place God has chosen for us.

We know that we live in a world that is full of suffering and sorrow, but also of great joy and the quiet happiness of loving relationships and good work done well. As a Christian each of us has been gifted by God with talents in order to make the world the place he intended: a place of mercy and love, sharing and care for all—where no one is too old, too poor, or too unimportant to count. Everyone is invited to the kingdom, and it is our job as disciples to make that an attractive prospect for others.

We are called to work out how we may best live our vocation as disciples in our lives and adapt as our circumstances change. Looking back at the four people with whom we began in the preface, we can see how each has a unique call. Roger, the physician, may have to change his work commitments, perhaps even taking a pay cut to have the time he needs with his family and community. Tom needs to see his daily work as a CEO as his Christian work. Marsha may have to cut back on parish work to be more active in her community. And Sandra needs support from her faith community in her difficult role as a politician.

Through regular prayer and the practices of humility, stewardship, and a life lived in balance, all of us can give the world and our neighbors a witness of life as we trust God to make use of us. The world needs us—both our work and our witness. Join the adventure of answering God's call in your life: in your family, your work, your community, and your parish. We need you!

Notes

1. Faith and Life *(pages 7–17)*

1. Thomas Aquinas, *Commentary on the Gospel of St. John* 1, trans. James A. Weisheipl (Albany, NY: Magi, 1980), 71.

2. Lucian, *The Death of Peregrine* in *The Works of Lucian of Samosata,* vol. 4, trans. H. W. Fowler and F. G. Fowler (Oxford: Clarendon, 1905), 82.

3. Paul Lakeland, "The Laity," in *From Trent to Vatican II: Historical and Theological Investigations,* ed. Raymond F. Bulman and Frederick J. Parrella (Oxford: Oxford University Press, 2006), 197.

4. Leon Joseph Cardinal Suenens, *The Gospel to Every Creature* (Westminster, MD: Newman, 1963), 19.

5. Ibid., 74–75.

6. Ibid., 22–23.

7. Harvey Cox, "The Market Is My Shepherd, and I Shall Want and Want and Want," *U.S. Catholic* (February 1, 2000), 38–42.

8. Pope Francis, Homily at Mass in Lampedusa, Italy (July 8, 2013), http://www.zenit.org/en/articles/pope-s-homily-at-mass-in-lampedusa.

2. God Calls Us in Scripture *(pages 18–38)*

1. Irenaeus, *Against the Heretics* 5, preface.

2. Dorothy L. Sayers, *The Mind of the Maker* (New York: HarperCollins, 1987), 22.

3. John R. Donahue and Daniel J. Harrington, *The Gospel of Mark,* Sacra Pagina 2 (Collegeville, MN: Liturgical Press, 2002), 17.

4. Gerald O'Mahony, *A Way in to the Trinity: The Story of a Journey* (Leominster, Herefordshire: Gracewing, 2004), 26–27.

5. Ambrose, *On the Christian Faith,* quoted in *Mark,* ed. Thomas C. Oden and Christopher A. Hall, Ancient Christian Commentary on Scripture: New Testament 2 (Downers Grove, IL: InterVarsity, 1988), 27.

6. Philip Van Linden, "Mark," in *The Collegeville Bible Commentary,* ed. Dianne Bergant and Robert J. Karris (Collegeville, MN: Liturgical Press, 1989), 914.

7. Donahue and Harrington, *The Gospel of Mark,* 234.

8. Donald Senior, *The Gospel of Matthew* (Nashville: Abingdon, 1997), 157.

3. Vatican II: The Council and the Laity *(pages 39–57)*

1. *L'Osservatore Romano,* Jan 26–27, 1959, qtd. in Yves Congar, "A Last Look at the Council," in *Vatican II Revisited by Those Who Were There,* ed. Alberic Stacpoole (Minneapolis: Winston, 1986), 337.

2. Joseph Ratzinger, *Theological Highlights of Vatican II* (Mahwah, NJ: Paulist, 1966), 23.

3. Congar, "A Last Look at the Council," 340.

4. Ratzinger, *Theological Highlights,* 31.

5. Ibid.

6. Yves M. J. Congar, *Lay People in the Church: A Study for a Theology of Laity,* trans. by Donald Attwater, revised ed. (Westminster, MD: The Newman Press, 1965), 17.

7. Ibid., 53.

8. Charles Moller, "History of the Constitution," in *Commentary on the Documents of Vatican II,* vol. 5, *Pastoral Constitution on the Church in the Modern World,* ed. Herbert Vorgrimler (New York: Herder & Herder, 1969), 11.

9. Ibid., 7.

10. Ibid., 44.

11. Ibid., 38.

12. Derek J. H. Worlock, " 'Toil in the Lord': The Laity in Vatican II," in *Vatican II Revisited by Those Who Were There,* 245.

13. For further information on witnessing in a postmodern world, see Don Everts and Doug Schaupp, *I Once Was Lost: What Postmodern Skeptics Taught Us about Their Path to Jesus* (Downers Grove, IL: InterVarsity, 2008), and Sherry A. Weddell, *Forming Intentional Disciples: The Path to Knowing and Following Jesus* (Huntington, IN: Our Sunday Visitor, 2012).

4. Discovering My Call *(pages 58–86)*

1. St. Irenaeus, *Against Heresies* V, preface, http://www.newadvent.org/fathers/0103500.htm.

2. Robert Bolton and Dorothy Grover Bolton, *People Styles at Work: Making Bad Relationships Good and Good Relationships Better* (New York: American Management Association, 1996), 24–25.

3. Nicholas W. Weiler and Stephen C. Schoonover, *Your Soul at Work: Five Steps to a More Fulfilling Career and Life* (Mahwah, NJ: HiddenSpring, 2001), 70–71.

4. Pope Francis, General Audience, June 5, 2013, http://w2.vatican.va/content/francesco/en/audiences/2013/documents/papa-francesco_20130605_udienza-generale.html.

5. This is a gross over-simplification, but it identifies an important transition in life. See Sharon Daloz Parks, *Big Questions, Worthy Dreams: Mentoring Emerging Adults in Their Search for Meaning, Purpose, and Faith* (San Francisco: Jossey-Bass, 2011), 91–93.

5. Living a 24/7 Christian Life *(pages 87–107)*

1. Jeff Haden, "10 Ways to Lose Friends and Irritate People," Yahoo! Small Business Advisor, April 16, 2014, https://smallbusiness.yahoo.com/advisor/10-ways-to-lose-friends-and-irritate-people-163429125.html.

2. C. S. Lewis, *The Screwtape Letters* (New York: HarperCollins, 1996), 112–13.

3. Ibid., 53–56.

4. Jim Collins, "The Triumph of Humility and Fierce Resolve," *Harvard Business Review* 83, no. 7/8 (July/August 2005), 136–46.

5. Pope Francis, General Audience, June 5, 2013, http://w2.vatican.va/content/francesco/en/audiences/2013/documents/papa-francesco_20130605_udienza-generale.html.

6. Thomas Lewis, Fari Amini, and Richard Lannon, *A General Theory of Love* (New York: Random House, 2000), 144, 191–92.

7. Anne-Marie Slaughter, "Why Women Still Can't Have It All," *Atlantic Monthly* (July/August 2012), http://www.theatlantic.com/magazine/archive/2012/07/why-women-still-cant-have-it-all/309020/.

6. Prayer *(pages 108–16)*

1. Kate Pickert, "The Mindful Revolution: The Science of Finding Focus in a Stress-Out Multitasking Culture," *Time*, February 3, 2014, 40–46.

2. Maxwell E. Johnson, ed., with the Monks of Saint John's Abbey, *Benedictine Daily Prayer: A Short Breviary* (Collegeville, MN: Liturgical Press, 2005).

3. The Catechism also includes the following citation: *Littera gesta docet, quid credas allegoria, moralis quid agas, quo tendas anagogia.* Augustine of Dacia, *Rotulus pugillaris,* I: ed. A. Walz: *Angelicum* 6 (1929) 256.

Bibliography

Thomas Aquinas, Saint. *Commentary on the Gospel of St John*, Part 1. Trans lated by James A. Weisheipl. Albany, NY: Magi, 1980.

Bergant, Dianne, and Robert J. Karris, ed. *The Collegeville Bible Commentary*. Collegeville, MN: Liturgical Press, 1989.

Collins, Jim. "The Triumph of Humility and Fierce Resolve," *Harvard Business Review* 83, no. 7/8 (July/August 2005): 136–46.

Congar, Yves. *Lay People in the Church: A Study for a Theology of Laity*. Translated by Donald Attwater. Revised edition. Westminster, MD: Newman, 1965.

Cox, Harvey. "The Market Is My Shepherd, and I Shall Want and Want and Want," *U.S. Catholic* (February 1, 2000): 38–42.

Donahue, John R., and Daniel J. Harrington. *The Gospel of Mark*. Sacra Pagina 2. Collegeville, MN: Liturgical Press, 2002.

Everts, Don, and Doug Schaupp. *I Once Was Lost: What Post-Modern Skeptics Taught Us About Their Path To Jesus*. Downers Grove, IL: InterVarsity, 2008.

Lakeland, Paul. "The Laity." In *From Trent to Vatican II: Historical and Theological Investigations*, edited by Raymond F. Bulman and Frederick J. Parrella, 193–208. New York: Oxford University Press, 2006.

Lewis, C. S. *The Screwtape Letters*. New York: HarperCollins, 1996.

Lewis, Thomas, Fari Amini, and Richard Lannon. *A General Theory of Love*. New York: Random House, 2000.

Moller, Charles. "History of the Constitution." In *Commentary on the Documents of Vatican II. Vol V. Pastoral Constitution on the Church in the Modern World,* edited by Herbert Vorgrimler, 1–77. New York: Herder & Herder, 1969.

Oden, Thomas C., and Christopher A. Hall, eds. *Mark*. Ancient Christian Commentary on Scripture: New Testament 2. Downers Grove, IL: InterVarsity, 1988.

O'Mahony, Gerald. A *Way in to the Trinity: The Story of a Journey*. Leominster, Herefordshire: Gracewing, 2004.

Ratzinger, Joseph. *Theological Highlights of Vatican II*. Mahwah, NJ: Paulist, 1966.

Rokeach, Milton. *The Nature of Human Values*. New York: The Free Press, 1973.

Sayers, Dorothy L. *The Mind of the Maker*. New York: HarperCollins, 1987.

Senior, Donald. *The Gospel of Matthew*. Nashville: Abingdon, 1997.

Stacpoole, Alberic, ed. *Vatican II Revisited by Those Who Were There*. Minneapolis: Winston, 1986.

Suenens, Leon Joseph. *The Gospel to Every Creature*. Westminster, MD: Newman, 1963.

Weddell, Sherry A. *Forming Intentional Disciples: The Path to Knowing and Following Jesus*. Huntington, IN: Our Sunday Visitor, 2012.